THE LAW OF SEPARATION AND DIVORCE

by PARNELL CALLAHAN

This legal Almanac has been revised by the Oceana Editorial Staff

Irving J. Sloan
General Editor

FOURTH EDITION

1979 Oceana Publications, Inc.
Dobbs Ferry, New York

Library of Congress in Publication Data

Callahan, Parnell Joseph Terence.
   The law of separation and divorce.

   (Legal almanac series; no. 1)
   1. Divorce—United   States—Popular   Works. 2. Separation
(Law)—United States—Popular Works. I. Title.
KF535.Z95C3   1978   346'.73'0166   78-25547
ISBN 0-379-11108-X

Manufactured in the United States of America

CONTENTS

Chapter I
ANTE-NUPTIAL AGREEMENTS 1

Chapter II
MARRIAGE 4

Chapter III
ANNULMENT 12

Chapter IV
SEPARATION 14

Chapter V
SEPARATION AGREEMENTS 18

Chapter VI
DIVORCE 22

Chapter VII
OUT-OF-STATE AND FOREIGN DIVORCES 31

Chapter VIII
REMARRIAGE 37

Chapter IX
ALIMONY AND PROPERTY RIGHTS 41

Chapter X
ENFORCEMENT AND MODIFICATION OF
    ALIMONY AWARDS 45

Chapter XI
MARRIAGES AND RIGHTS OF MILITARY
    PERSONNEL 50

Chapter XII
PROCEDURE FOR OBTAINING AN ANNULMENT,
    SEPARATION OR DIVORCE 55

Appendix A
LEGAL AGE FOR MARRIAGE AND LICENSE
    REQUIREMENTS 61

Appendix B
DEGREES OF RELATIONSHIP WITHIN WHICH
    MARRIAGES ARE PROHIBITED 64

Appendix C
STATUTORY REQUIREMENTS TO CREATE A VALID
   MARRIAGE 72

Appendix D
AGE OF CONSENT FOR MARRIAGE 77

Appendix E
SUMMARY OF DIVORCE LAWS BY STATE 79

GLOSSARY 117

INDEX 123

Chapter I

ANTE-NUPTIAL AGREEMENTS

Quite often persons who are about to marry consider the regulation before marriage of rights in inheritance and property. There are, of course, certain rights which may not be waived and obligations which may not be the grounds for relief since agreements with respect to them may violate the public policy of the State. For example, in most States a wife may not waive her right to support as long as she remains a wife. This is usually so whether an agreement dealing with support is made before or after marriage. Thus an agreement between a woman and a man who are engaged to be married that in the event of a divorce there will be no alimony will usually be held to be unenforceable as against the public policy of the State.

An ante-nuptial agreement or contract is a contract, as its name implies, made before marriage and in contemplation of marriage. The contracts are usually entered into in consideration of marriage and marriage itself is sufficient "consideration." (See Legal Almanac No. 36--The Law of Contracts--to sustain the validity of a contract.) In an ante-nuptial contract or agreement or in an ante-nuptial settlement, the property rights and interests of either the prospective husband or wife or both are determined and property may be secured to either or both of the parties or to their children by prior marriages or to the children to be born to them of their marriage.

In general, the requirements for the validity of an ante-nuptial contract are the same as those for the validity of any other contract. The parties must have the capacity to understand what they are doing, there must be consideration for the promises or acts of each party (marriage alone will be sufficient consideration), the agreement must be free from any type of misrepresentation, fraud or undue influence, and each of the parties must be of sufficient age to enter into a contract.

If either of the parties is under age, the other party runs the risk of the underage partner exercising his or her right to disaffirm the contract after reaching legal age.

In order to be valid, an ante-nuptial contract or agreement, in addition to satisfying the other requirements of the law of contracts, must encourage the preservation of the marriage. An ante-nuptial agreement to the effect that a husband and wife will separate after marriage, or that they will not live together as husband and wife at any time after the marriage, or that they will obtain a divorce within the stated period after marriage, or at the expiration or happening of certain events, will almost universally be held void as against public policy and as promoting divorce rather than as encouraging and sustaining the solidarity of the prospective family and the success of the anticipated marriage.

If a prospective husband and wife anticipating the birth of a child within six months after marriage agree to separate immediately after the ceremony and to provide for a divorce after the birth of the child or to provide for an annulment or to relieve the husband of the obligation of supporting the wife and child, the contract will not be sustained since it obviously is against public policy. Almost any ante-nuptial agreement providing for the waiver of alimony in the event of a separation or divorce will be held void, although a recitation in a contract to the effect that the wife has certain means and will limit her demands for alimony or support in the event of a separation may be upheld if the figures are accurate and reasonable.

Some states provide specifically by statute for ante-nuptial contracts and in almost all states such agreements must be in writing in order to avoid a violation of the "Statute of Frauds," a term which is of considerable importance and which is explained in greater detail in Legal Almanac No. 36.

Typical situations in which ante-nuptial agreements are used are those in which a woman of considerable wealth is marrying a man in less fortunate circumstances and where some of her money is tied up in trust funds or where both parties want the assurance that the marriage is for love and not for gold. In such circumstances, the husband will waive his rights to elect against her will to take his intestate share (see Legal Almanac No. 33--

The Law of Inheritance for greater details). Other instances are where both parties have been married before and desire to protect the rights of inheritance of their children by former marriages and where, having some material possessions in their separate names, they desire to place certain property in joint names or joint possession and to retain their separate and distinct interests in other property (see also Legal Almanacs No. 2--How to Make a Will--No. 46--Legal Status of Young Adults--No. 53--Legal Status of Women--and No. 45--Law for the Family Man) and to provide that each will bequeath or devise a certain amount of property in specified proportions to children to be born of the anticipated marriage.

Many marriages which might have been unhappy have been avoided by the presentation of an ante-nuptial agreement which may have considerable effect in insuring that spouses marry for each other and not for the material wealth or benefits of the anticipated spouse.

In some countries of the world an ante-nuptial agreement is mandatory before the performance of a marriage ceremony and both the conduct of the prospective spouses as well as the regulation of their property must be defined in their agreement and reduced to writing.

3

Chapter II
MARRIAGE

The Constitution of the United States has left to the various states of the union complete authority over legislation concerning marriage and divorce. Therefore, the laws of marriage and divorce vary from state to state. Until September 1, 1967, New York granted a divorce on only one ground--adultery, while other states recognized many more, with the examples of Rhode Island with 13 grounds and Nevada with 10 grounds. This variance in laws may cause complications which are beyond the scope of this Almanac and emphasize the necessity of your consulting your lawyer. This Almanac can serve at best as an introduction to your legal rights and as an indication of the questions which you must ask your lawyer, and which he probably will ask you.

Marriage has been defined as " . . . the civil status condition or relation of one man and one woman united in law, for the discharge to each other and the community of the duties legally incumbent on those whose association is founded on the distinction of sex . . ." A marriage can be performed only between a man and a woman. Marriage has also been defined as "a contract according to the form prescribed by laws by which a man and woman capable of entering into such a contract, mutually engaged with each other to live their whole lives together in the state of union which ought to exist between a husband and wife."

Marriage is for life--or until a Court terminates the status and relationship. Marriage cannot be performed for a period of time or a period of years.

The domestic relation laws of most states and particularly of the State of New York define marriage as " . . . a civil contract to which the consent of the parties is essential . . . ." To the concept of marriage as a "civil contract" the Courts have added the element of status to which the state is a third party.

The basic element in the creation of any marriage is "con-

4

sent." Without consent, there can be no valid marriage. However, consent will not suffice to make a marriage valid. Since the state is a party to the marriage contract, and since marriage is a social institution in which the state has an interest and in which the "public policy of the state is involved, the state has the power to require that various conditions in and addition to consent, be met before the state will recognize the existence of a valid marriage."

Broadly speaking, it is possible for a marriage to take place by one of three methods:

    a. a marriage based upon the consent of the parties, the issuance of the marriage license and the performance of a marriage ceremony by a civil officer authorized to perform marriage ceremonies or by a duly ordained, or authorized clergyman (a religious ceremony is required only in Delaware and Maryland).

    b. the execution by the parties of a formal written contract of marriage which thereafter is filed in the office of the county clerk.

    c. a marriage based on the consent of the parties, cohabitation of the parties as husband and wife, and the parties holding themselves out to the general public as husband and wife.

Marriages performed by a duly authorized official after the issuance of the license, are recognized in all states as long as they do not fall in one of the prohibited categories. In most states a marriage performed without a license, and not within a prohibited relationship or status is valid although the person or official performing the ceremony may be subject to a penalty or fine.

Marriage by contract is a seldom-used form of marriage, and is permitted in only a few states. In such states, a formal marriage ceremony is not required but after the issuance of a license, a couple may sign an agreement contracting marriage. Their signatures must be affixed to the document before a notary public who will authenticate their signatures, and thereafter the agreement must be filed in the office of the county clerk.

In the United States, there are very few cases on record where such a marriage ceremony or formula is utilized although it is comparatively frequent in some European, African or Asiatic countries, particularly in some Arab countries where the bride does not attend the wedding and where the contract is signed for her by her father.

Common Law Marriages

A common law marriage is a marriage without a ceremony of any sort. It occurs where a man and a woman live together as a spouse and where, in addition to their mutual recognition they hold themselves out to the public as man and wife. The number of States recognizing such marriage is shrinking, and today in most States common law marriages entered into at the present time will not be recognized. Some states recognize them if entered into before certain dates while other states do not recognize them at all.

TABLE I

States which recognize Common Law Marriages

Alaska		
Alabama	Iowa	Pennsylvania
Colorado	*Kansas	Rhode Island
Florida	Montana	South Carolina
Georgia	Ohio	Texas
Idaho	Oklahoma	District of Columbia

TABLE II

States in which Common Law Marriages are
Recognized Conditionally

California	(if entered into before 1895)
Indiana	(if entered into before January 1, 1958
Michigan	(if entered into before January 1, 1957)
Mississippi	(if entered into before April 5, 1956)

*But the parties are subject to punishment for not obtaining a license.

TABLE II (continued)

Missouri	(if entered into before March 31, 1921)
Nebraska	(if entered into before March 31, 1921)
New Jersey	(if entered into before December 1, 1939)
New York	(if entered into before April 29, 1933)
South Dakota	(if entered into before July 1, 1959)

TABLE III

States which do not recognize Common Law Marriage

Arizona	Arkansas	California
Connecticut	Delaware	Hawaii
Illinois	*Kentucky	Louisiana
Maryland	Massachusetts	New Hampshire
New Mexico	North Carolina	North Dakota
Oregon	Tennessee	Utah
Vermont	Virginia	Washington
West Virginia	Wisconsin	Wyoming
Maine	Puerto Rico	Nevada

Many States, although prohibiting common law marriages of their own residents and refusing to recognize them, will recognize common law marriages if the common law marriages were contracted in a State where they are recognized as valid or if there was cohabitation as husband and wife and a presentation to the world or to the public, as husband and wife while physically present in a State recognizing such relationships.

Restraints Upon Marriage

Almost all States recognize certain disabilities or legal impediments to marriage. These may have the effect of making the marriage completely void, or merely voidable. A completely

*In Kentucky, common law marriages are valid only for the purposes of the Workmen's Compansation Law.

7

void marriage, as for example between a brother and a sister, cannot be validated for any purpose or under any circumstances. A voidable marriage, such as one involving an infant or person under the age of consent, is valid until its validity is attacked in a Court and a judgment declaring it to be invalid is entered. Insofar as a void marriage is concerned, however, as a general rule, no decree is necessary to set it aside since it was never valid.

Void Marriages

In most States the following disabilities will result in a marriage being void:

1. Either party contracted a prior marriage still existing at the time of the subsequent marriage.

2. The parties are related to each other by birth or marriage, within certain prohibited degrees. These marriages are termed incestuous and therefore void.

3. One or both of the parties is an adjudged incompetent, lunatic or idiot (in some States such marriages are voidable but not void, and in some States they may be ratified by a lunatic or incompetent who is restored to his full senses).

Voidable Marriages

Voidable marriages (see Chapter III) generally require an action for an annulment or for a declaratory judgment to declare them invalid. They may result from the disabilities set forth below, or from some other ground. In order to set aside or invalidate a voidable marriage, the party suffering from the disability, or against whom some fraud or duress has been practiced, may bring an action for an annulment. In the case of an incompetent or insane person, the action may be brought by his legal representative and in the case of a person who is deceased, his personal representative, executor or administrator, may bring the action even after his or her death. This is usually done when property rights are involved.

The following disabilities may create a voidable marriage:

1. Either or both parties under the age of consent.

2. Either or both parties lacking the understanding to con-

sent to a marriage.

3. Either party physically incapable of engaging in sexual intercourse.

4. The consent of either party was obtained through fraud, duress or force.

In order to constitute a ground for declaring a marriage void, the disabilities or conditions must have existed at the time of the marriage ceremony.

Tables V and VI, at the end of this chapter indicate the States which have statutory provisions imposing restraints upon marriage by reason of family relationship (blood or marriage) or by reasons of race (no longer enforcible).

Age of Consent

Where either or both parties are below the age of consent, the marriage may be void or voidable, depending on the age of the infant. If the party contracting or attempting to contract marriage is so young as to require the protection of the law, the State, in the exercise of its public policy, may declare the marriage to be completely void. In most States there is one age at which a marriage is absolutely prohibited and at which it will be declared void, and another age at which a marriage may be performed with parental consent and where, if performed without parental consent, it will be only voidable, and not absolutely void.

All States specify the ages below which persons may not marry, and the ages at which they may marry with parental consent. In many states, however, the age limits may be disregarded in the best interests of the minors, particularly where the bride is pregnant.

Consanguinity

Where the parties are related by birth or marriage within certain prohibited degrees of consanguinity, or relationship, as specified in the law of the State where the marriage occurred, no valid marriage may be contracted. (See Table V at the end of this chapter.)

All States prohibit marriages between a person and his or her:

9

A. Mother or father;
B. Daughter or son;
C. Grandmother or grandfather;
D. Granddaughter or grandson;
E. Aunt or uncle;
F. Sister or brother;
G. Niece or nephew.

Some states prohibit marriage between first cousins of the whole or half blood. You should consult a lawyer for the law applicable in your own particular jurisdiction, since laws change and Court decisions may affect the binding effect of a statute.

Mixed Marriages

While several States have laws against mixed marriages, i.e., between persons of Caucasian race and persons of the Negro, Oriental or Indian races, the United States Supreme Court has held such laws unconstitutional. Effectively, therefore, there are now no restrictions against such marriages.

Generally, the prohibitions of the statutes are effective to the third generation inclusive, with regard to the descendants of Negroes, Orientals, American Indians or Eskimos, and many State Legislatures have specifically stated that marriage between a white person and a person of one-third or more Negro blood is prohibited. These marriages, if performed in violation of the statute, are usually void. At least one State, California, has declared unconstitutional a statute prohibiting interracial marriages.

The Marriage Ceremony

Despite the mandates in the United States Constitution regulating the separation of church and state and the freedom of religion, Delaware and Maryland require a religious ceremony. In all States, any duly ordained clergyman of a recognized sect is empowered to perform a marriage ceremony, while in most States numerous other officials such as Judges of various courts, Justices of the Peace, Mayors, Recorders, City and Police Ma-

10

gistrates, and City Clerks are also designated to perform marriages. Almost all States have enacted statutes providing for the recording of marriages. Marriage licenses may be issued by various officials such as County Clerks, Recorders, Registrars of Vital Statistics and others, depending upon the local and State regulations. Some States have statutes permitting the solemnization of marriages by Quaker and Baha'i Faiths, where no clergymen actually participate.

However, the ceremony may not take place less than 24 hours after the marriage license has been issued, and may not take place less than three days after the date of the physical or serological examination.

As a general rule, the State laws do not require any specific or particular words. As long as the parties declare solemnly that they take each other as husband and wife and make this declaration in the presence of the individual performing the ceremony and two or more witnesses the ceremony is legal. Some States require more witnesses than others.

Chapter III
ANNULMENT

In the preceding Chapter, we have discussed legel impediments or disabilities which may have the effect of making a marriage either void or voidable. In the case of a void marriage,
some States do not require any action whatsoever, while others
insist upon a Court decree stating to the world and particularly
as between the parties that the marriage is void. A declaration
of nullity or a judgment holding the marriage to be void may be
obtained either by one of the parties, or in the case of an incompetent person, by his Committee or Guardian. In the case of
death of one of the parties, where estate rights are involved, the
Executor, Administrator, relatives, or even the heirs of the deceased party may bring the action for a declaration that the marriage is void.

While there is a difference of opinion, and a difference in
the laws of the various States as to the necessity for a declaration of nullity of a void marriage, a voidable marriage remains
a valid marriage until one of the parties has obtained a judgment
declaring it a nullity or having it set aside. Generally speaking,
a marriage otherwise valid and without a legal impediment may
be annulled on the suit of one of the parties to the marriage.
Annulments may be granted for the following grounds:

1. Non-age of the party suing for the annulment (but only
if the party has not lived with or cohabited with the other spouse
after attaining the age at which a valid marriage may be contracted without parental consent).

2. Idiocy, lunacy or incapacity at the time of the marriage
(provided the party who is so disabled did not live with the other
party after regaining his full mental capacity).

3. Physical incapacity where one of the parties is unable
to consummate the marriage (this refers to marital relations and

not the ability to bear or beget children), and where the injured party did not know of the incapacity at the time of the marriage or did not know that it wasn't curable.

4. Consent to the marriage obtained by force or duress (provided that the party against whom the force or duress was used did not voluntarily cohabit or continue to live with the other party after the actual force or duress was passed).

5. Fraud. This may consist of concealment of a previous marriage or divorce, concealment of chastity, concealment or misrepresentation of financial condition, concealment of pregnancy, concealment of disease, misrepresentation of character or of prior civilian or military record, refusal to have children, or refusal to engage in a religious ceremony after the civil ceremony.

If the injured party continues to reside with the other spouse after learning of the fraud, the fraud may be held to have been condoned.

When we speak of the "grounds for an annulment" we refer to grounds for declarations of nullity of void marriages as well as for the annulment and termination of voidable marriages.

The question of "Fraud" may include many fact patterns. A detailed discussion of the fraud which will permit the annulment of a marriage is beyond the scope of this Almanac. The permissible grounds of fraud, and the extent to which fraud must have been practiced to authorize the annulment of a marriage vary not only from State to State, but also within the same State, where Courts of some areas of a state are more lenient or more strict than Courts in another area.

Chapter IV

SEPARATION

There are two kinds of "Legal Separations"--a separation by agreement, and a separation by judgment of a Court. Both are often referred to indiscriminately as a "separation" or "legal separation." A separation agreement is not a judgment, although it may be incorporated into a judgment of separation or a judgment of divorce. If one party violates the agreement and the other party wishes legal redress, he or she must start a court proceeding in order to compel compliance with the separation agreement. A breach or violation of a judgment of separation, however, may be enforced in the subsequent action by a separate proceeding or "motion" subsequent to trial.

Violation of the terms of a separation agreement will permit the aggrieved spouse to sue for damages for breach of the agreement. However, violation of a separation judgment will subject the violator to punishment by the Court for a contempt of Court, and may result in a fine or commitment to the Civil Jail.

A separation, whether by agreement or by judgment of separation, differs both from a divorce and an annulment in that the parties, while separated from bed and board, are still married to each other and are not freed from the bonds of matrimony. Neither is free to marry any other person. A husband and wife may agree to separate, and may merely move into separate homes without any formal written agreement. On the other hand, they may sign a formal separation agreement, consenting to live separate and apart, providing for the distribution of their joint property, and providing for the support of the wife and children of the marriage. A separation agreement, whether informal and oral, may be terminated by another formal document or by the action of the parties in moving back together and re-

14

suming cohabitation as husband and wife.

A judgment of separation, however, may be terminated only by another judgment or order of the court. The fact that a husband and wife resume living together will not affect the permanency of this judgment of separation, although it will suspend provisions for payment as long as the husband and wife live together and support is provided, even if the amount of support is less than that called for by the agreement.

In some states, either party to a judgment of separation may ask the Court to vacate the judgment on the grounds that the parties have reconciled in fact, while in other states the judgment of separation remains in effect until both parties have joined in asking the Court to set aside, nullify or vacate the judgment.

In almost all states, an action or suit for a separation may be begun by either the husband or the wife. While separation actions are begun by the party claiming to be innocent, there have been instances in which a husband has admitted his fault and has asked the Court to give his wife a separation on the grounds of his own misconduct, in order to determine his liability for support and to fix the amount of his obligations. A separation action or suit may be brought for a permanent separation or for a seperation for a limited period of time. The most common grounds are abandonment, cruel and inhuman conduct and non-support. As a rule, an action for a separation will not bar the complaining party from later bringing an action for absolute divorce on the same or additional grounds, and in some states a separation judgment may be converted into a divorce after a period of years. In other states, however, a judgment of separation is held to be an "election of remedies" which will bar a suit for a divorce on the same grounds. This is another area in which the advice of a lawyer is essential.

Other states permit either party to a separation agreement to sue for a divorce on the grounds of living separate and apart pursuant to an agreement, after a certain period of time has elapsed subsequent to the execution of the agreement and the filing of the agreement in the County Clerk's office.

A judgment of separation sanctions and judicially approves as justified the refusal of one spouse to cohabit with the other, and the spouse in whose favor such a judgment has been granted may not thereafter be sued for either a separation or a divorce for other acts of misconduct, if not waived in the agreement, whether such acts were committed before or after the agreement.

In this connection, a judgment of divorce granted after a judgment of separation, or after the filing of a separation agreement is often referred to as the "conversion decree." A wife should be extremely cautious in instituting an action for a separation, since in some states the guilty spouse, who has been adjudicated by the judgment of separation to have been at fault, may nevertheless sue for a divorce and may extinguish or limit the innocent wife's right to inheritance from the guilty husband.

In some states there is no action for a separation but only for an absolute divorce or annulment. There may be practical reasons why an injured spouse may not want a divorce to be granted. For example, a divorced husband may remarry and assume new financial obligations which increase the difficulty of enforcing the payment of alimony and child support. No layman should attempt to act in this area without the advice of a competent attorney, to whom he should reveal all the relevant facts.

It should be noted that many states which recognize the grounds of desertion, habitual drunkenness, habitual use of drugs, and non-support, as well as living separate and apart, require the ground upon which the complaint is based to have been a continuing condition.

Grounds for divorce and separation are often similar, although as a general rule a greater degree of proof is required for the granting of a divorce than for a separation. Abandonment, for example, may not be the same as desertion, and what is "cruelty" in one state may not qualify as "cruel and inhuman treatment," or as "intolerable cruelty" in another.

Chapter V

SEPARATION AGREEMENTS

Under the old English Common Law, a married woman could not enter into a contract. Any agreements which she made with her husband violated this rule because as far as contractual rights were concerned, she and her husband were regarded as one person. However, in 1718 an English Court held that a separate agreement between a husband and a wife was binding, and at the present time in the United States and England it is almost universally held that separation agreements or separation contracts between husband and wife, if not made as part of an agreement to obtain a divorce, as opposed to a separation agreement between a husband and wife, settling the property rights of the parties, providing for the maintenance of the wife and the children, and releasing claims by the spouses on each other's property and estate, will usually be held valid as long as there is no manifest unfairness in the agreement, and as long as the agreement does not violate the public policy of the state.

Under no circumstances should one lawyer represent both spouses. Despite mutual trust of an attorney, agreements can be set aside if a party did not have the benefit of independent representation by the counsel of his or her own choice. Separation agreements require the utmost good faith on the part of both spouses, and a higher degree of good faith on the part of the husband. Both parties must disclose all facts and the wife must act freely, of her own accord, and not under financial, emotional or family pressure or abuse.

A formal written document is usually required, and an infant may not sign a separation agreement without approval of the Court. Such a separation agreement is voidable by the infant after obtaining majority as long as it has not been ratified after majority.

18

Insofar as provisions for support of the children are concerned, they are seldom held to be binding on the children. The Uniform Support of Dependents Law, and the Family Courts Act enacted in most of the states permit a Court to award support for children greater than that provided in a separation agreement, in the event of a change of circumstances involving an improvement of the financial position of the husband, or an increase in the needs of the children.

The separation agreement itself may be a rather simple document or it may be considerably involved. While it is replete with legal terms such as "whereas" and "Witnesseth," the present tendency is to simplify the agreements and to reduce them to language which the parties who are not lawyers can understand. A modern form of agreement is printed in the appendix, with language simplified so it can be understood and obeyed without consulting a lawyer a second time (you should, of course, consult your lawyer, and have him explain the agreement before you sign it. However, you should never attempt to draw an agreement yourself and you should retain the services and advice of a lawyer, practicing in the state where the agreement is to be signed and where the parties reside. If the parties reside in different states, the lawyers will recognize that.

It is not the function of this legal almanac to explain in detail the different paragraphs, clauses and articles of separation agreements. The subject of separation agreements will be covered in another volume of the legal almanac series to be published later this year.

A local attorney should also be consulted as to the requirements of filing the agreement. While most states and jurisdictions do not require the agreement to be filed, in some states the agreement itself will not be recognized unless it has been filed, and in other states the filing is a prerequisite to a divorce on the grounds of separation. In New York, for example, the new divorce law to become effective September 1, 1967, permits either party to a separation agreement to apply for a divorce after the parties have been living separate and apart for two years pursuant to the terms of a separation agreement which has been executed and asknowledged by both parties and filed in the office of the County Clerk of a county in which one of the parties resides within 30 days after the execution of the agreement.

This is one area in which you should not attempt to dispense with the advice of a lawyer. For a valid separation agreement, both parties should be represented by lawyers selected independently of the other spouse.

Effect of Reconciliation

After a husband and wife have separated physically from each other, and after their physical separation, have signed a formal written separation agreement, they may desire to reconcile or resume cohabitation. As a general rule, a reconciliation will revoke a separation agreement. Most lawyers try to avoid the effect of this automatic revocation by having a clause in the separation agreement providing that the agreement remains in full force and effect whether the parties live separate and apart, or whether they resume living together on an "occasional," "casual," "extended" or permanent basis. However, since the public policy of all states of the United States encourages reconciliation, and the preservation of family solidarity, most provisions in agreements providing for the continuance of a status of separation after the parties have in fact reconciled are held to be ineffective and contrary to the public policy of the State.

While one night spent under the same roof or even in the same bed may not be sufficient to effect a revocation of a separation agreement, it may be sufficient if on that one night the husband and wife agreed that they would resume living together and that their separation would be a thing of the past. In each case, it is a matter of intent, to be determined by the Judge or jury who is trying the case.

If a separation agreement has been entered into, both a husband and a wife should be careful to safeguard their legal rights and the obligations of the other spouse. It may be necessary for them to undergo for a second time the agony of a separation, and court proceedings leading to a second separation agreement, or they may, on the part of at least one spouse, unwittingly and unwillingly revoke an agreement and subject themselves to the necessity of and the liability to another court action for a separation.

Very often, this problem has been solved by the husband and wife consenting to the entry of a separation decree. A sepa-

20

ration decree will usually remain in effect even if the parties go back together, live together with the idea of making their reconciliation permanent. While they are together, the provisions of a separation judgment are suspended, but if they separate again, the judgment automatically goes into effect and each party is required to obey the terms of the judgment of separation.

There is no general rule as to what constitutes a reconciliation sufficient to invalidate the agreement. It is largely a matter of state of mind, and each case will usually be judged on its own facts. Under the circumstances, this is another area where a husband and wife should consult lawyers, to be sure that they accomplish legally and properly whatever they have in mind.

Cost of a Separation Agreement

The fees of lawyers for drawing separation agreements vary not only from State to State, but in different areas within the same County or City. In order to avoid a misunderstanding, you should discuss with your lawyer the matter of his fees and his charges. He may not be able to give you a definite charge or fee for the drawing of an agreement since it may require some negotiation or research. Usually, the husband pays the fees of the wife's lawyer as well as those of his own lawyer. However, in the case of a wealthy wife and an impecunious husband, the wife may pay her own fees.

Most local Bar Associations maintain Minimum Fee Schedules to which lawyers are required to adhere. Fees vary greatly above these minimum charges, and you should attempt to arrive at a clear understanding with your lawyer as soon as possible. It is customary to pay a retaining fee or advance payment of the total fee as soon as the lawyer is actually "retained" or hired.

21

Chapter VI
DIVORCE

The subject of divorce is extremely complicated and no one without extensive legal training should attempt to solve his marital problems without the advice of an attorney. Even among attorneys, the changing laws, statutes, court decisions and regulations, as well as local ground rules, require constant study to keep abreast of changes and developments.

This advice is essential, not only after a person has been served with a summons, but at any time when he or she contemplates a divorce or when his or her spouse contemplates a divorce.

A person may have a residence in more than one state, and since the rights and liabilities of spouses vary with states, the choice of a state is extremely important. The relief to be granted may depend on whether there has been a personal appearance or an appearance by attorney representing the defendant. This may present a problem of conflict of laws which is beyond the scope of this almanac. Do not attempt to use this book as a substitute for the advice of your attorney. A perusal of this book, however, will prepare you for the questions which your attorney must ask you to defend or prosecute your case.

Residence Requirements

All states have a minimum period during which a person is required to be a continuous resident before filing suit for a divorce. This requirement is primarily to discourage, or to encourage residents of foreign states, who sometimes shop for a jurisdiction recognizing a ground not permitted in the state of original residence. For example, until September 1, 1967, New York did not grant a divorce on any ground other than adultery. If no adultery has been committed, or if the innocent spouse does not want to stigmatize the guilty spouse, the innocent spouse may move to another state and after completing the residence requirements, and after being advised by an attorney of the state of new residence, (as well as by an attorney in the state from which he has departed) may in most cases institute an action on grounds recognized in the state of his new residence. Some states, however, limit certain grounds to acts committed or situations arising after the acquisition of the new residence.

While Appendix E sets forth the times of residence required in the various states and territories, it does not purport to cover the entire law on the subject. Different rules may apply where the marriage was solemnized within the state or where both parties were always residents of the state. Appendix E refers primarily to limitations set by states against persons who are not original bona fide residents of the state, and who may be seeking merely to take advantage of the state's divorce laws by establishing a new residence.

Most of the states have the residence requirements similar to divorce requirements for the institution of a separation or annulment action.

It should be noted that residence requirements may not necessarily apply where the ground for divorce is insanity occurring subsequent to the marriage. Because of the unusual nature of these grounds, many states require proof of residence for the same period that the insanity must exist before it is considered a cause for an absolute divorce. For example, if the insanity has existed for two years, but the state requires only a one-year residence for the commencement of a divorce action, the state may nevertheless require a two-year residence during which the insanity continued before permitting the commencement of an action for divorce on the grounds of insanity.

In other states, the residence requirements differ according to the ground for the action and according to whether the cause of action or grounds are those within or without the state in which the divorce is begun.

Some states credit the time served in the armed forces toward the required residence period, but this again will depend upon the military law or the Soldiers & Sailors Civil Relief Act of 1940 as enacted and amended by Congress.

Although complaints in divorce actions differ from state to state, there are certain basic similarities. The complaint must always state (a) the date and place of the marriage; (b) the names and ages of the children; (c) the residence of the plaintiff in the state in which the action is brought; (d) the length of the time such residence has continued; (e) facts or grounds on which the cause of the action is based; and (f) the assertion that the action is not barred by the passage of time subsequent to the commission of the wrongful acts or the discovery by the plaintiff of the commission of the wrongful acts. Other states require a statement that the plaintiff has not forgiven or condoned the cause of action, and still others a statement that the plaintiff has not cohabited voluntarily with the defendant since the discovery of the grounds. Most states require a further statement that no decree of divorce has been obtained by either party against the other, and that no other action for a divorce is pending.

In cases where the wife is the plaintiff and there are no children, she may consider asking that she be permitted to resume her maiden name and if this relief is granted to her, a provision to that effect may be included in the decree or judgment of divorce.

In almost all states, the complaint must be sworn to but in many states the defendant is permitted to serve an answer which is unknown, particularly where the grounds for the divorce are also a violation of the criminal code or penal laws of the state, (see Legal Almanac No. 9 "Legal Regulation of Sexual Conduct") such as adultery or felonious assault.

While each of the states has its own divorce law, and while the District of Columbia code and the laws governing territories provide additional divorce laws, there has been a great deal of simplification within the last fifty years. In the early history of the United States, a divorce required the passage of a special law or act by the State Legislature for each separate divorce. As more divorces were desired, the State Legislatures enacted codes permitting divorces on specified grounds, thus eliminating legislation which was in effect private rather than public.

A large percentage of divorces are "amicable" with questions of property and support prearranged before the actual appearance in court. In such circumstances, the divorce proof is "pro forma" or formal and the agreement between the parties, after being scrutinized by the Court, particularly in cases where the support of children is involved, is incorporated into the judgment of divorce, with the consent of the parties and the approval of the Court.

The grounds upon which the various states will grant divorces are set forth in Appendix E.

Where a divorce has been obtained outside of the State of permanent residence, with no fraud against either party or against the rendering state, the Courts of all other states are bound to recognize this divorce under the full faith and credit clause of the Constitution of the United States.

Grounds for Divorce

Several technical rules concerning divorce grounds must be mentioned at the outset. In the first place grounds are exclusively statutory. If the conduct alleged does not fit into one of the statutory categories of grounds, the divorce may not be granted. Secondly, generally speaking the law of the state is that which will be applied in determining whether the divorce will be granted -- that is, the state in which the divorce action is being brought (the "forum"). This is true even though the conduct relied upon as grounds for divorce occurred in another state. Finally, when the statutes governing grounds for divorce are amended, most courts hold that the new statute may be retroactively applied to conduct taking place before the amendment.

1. Adultery

Adultery is ground for divorce in most states, but it accounts for only a small proportion of the divorces granted. It is defined as the voluntary sexual intercourse of a married person with a person other than the spouse. When a married woman is raped, that is not adultery, since not voluntary. Homosexual contacts have been held not to be adultery.

A few cases have maintained that artificial insemination by a donor other than the husband (AID) constitutes adultery on the wife's part. But many states now have legislation which eliminate this interpretation where the husband consents to the process.

The major problem with the ground of adultery is that of proving the occurrence. Circumstantial evidence must necessarily be relied upon in most cases.

2. Desertion

Desertion as a ground for divorce is more important statistically than adultery. It is a ground for divorce in most states, under some statutes being called abandonment. It is defined as being (a) the voluntary separation by one spouse from the other, (b) with the intent not to resume marital cohabitation, (c) without the consent of the other spouse and (d) without justification.

Most of the desertion statutes impose the additional requirement that some specified period of time must elapse after the desertion may ripen into a ground for divorce. This period is most commonly a year but can be as long as five years under a few statutes. The period must be uninterrupted, runs from the moment of desertion, and usually must exclude time spent in prior marital litigation between the parties, and the time during which they lived apart under a prior separation decree. If the defendant leaves the home under circumstances not amounting to desertion, as where he intends to return, the period begins to run when the intent not to return is formed. A reconciliation will interrupt the running of the period. If an offer of reconciliation is made in good faith by the deserter, it has the effect of stopping the running of the period, and if it is unjustifiably refused, constitutes desertion by the other spouse.

It does not constitute desertion when the separation is agreed to by the spouses. But if after the desertion occurs, the deserted spouse makes an agreement concerning alimony or property which does not amount to the desertion, a right of action for the divorce is not affected.

Many cases have had to define the term "separation" as used in the context of desertion. When one of the spouses does not leave the marital home, but withdraws from association with

26

the other, is that desertion? Or when one spouse refuses to engage in sexual relations with the other, is that desertion? While the cases are not in agreement, desertion or abandonment has been defined as being the refusal to fulfill a basic obligation of the marriage. Hence the previous examples would suggest that desertion is involved.

3. Cruelty

Cruelty is a ground for divorce in all but a handful of states and is heavily relied upon. The divorce statutes of the various states which have cruelty as a ground for divorce make it plain that they require quite severe conduct, by adding such adjectives as "intolerable", "inhuman", "extreme", "grievous" or "barbarous". Some of them go on to define cruelty. New Jersey does this, for example, by describing it as "any physical or mental cruelty which endangers the safety or health of the plaintiff or makes it improper or unreasonable to expect the plaintiff to continue to cohabit with the defendant." The New York and Wisconsin statutes speak of "cruel and inhuman treatment." At least one state, South Carolina, limits the offense to physical cruelty. A few states also have the ground of indignities, which seem substantially similar to cruelty. Minnesota has recently substituted for cruelty a ground defined as "a course of conduct detrimental to the marriage relationship of the party seeking the divorce."

Some elements of the charge of cruelty which appear to be required in the cases are: (a) Cruelty generally must consist of a course of conduct over a period. A single act of cruelty is not sufficient grounds for divorce, except in the rare cases in which the act is outrageous or shocking or very brutal. (b) The plaintiff must prove that the cruelty had some effect upon his or her health before it will be held to be a ground for divorce. (c) The cases are divided as to whether the defendant's state of mind is relevant as to whether he has been guilty of cruelty. (d) To some degree at least, the cruelty is to be judged by its effect upon the individual plaintiff, with his or her sensibilities and weaknesses, not upon some mythical reasonable person.

Perhaps the most common form of cruelty consists of what might be characterized as general marital unkindness. This includes abuse, quarreling, harrassment, ridicule, refusal to speak to the spouse, accusations of infidelity or other misconduct, abuse of the children, attempts to alienate the children from the spouse and similar conduct.

27

Drug addiction and heavy drinking may also support a finding of cruelty. Various conduct relating to sexual relations may be found to be cruelty. Examples are refusal to have intercourse and "excessive" or "abnormal" demands.

4. Living Separate and Apart

This is a ground for divorce in about half of the states. It is to be distinguished from desertion in that it does not require evidence that one party departed from the marital domicile without justification, but only that the parties lived apart for a prescribed period, with certain qualifications depending upon the statutory language. The period specified by the statutes ranges from six months to five years, the most common being three or five years.

There are three types of statute authorizing divorce for separation, the proof required varying with the different language of the statute. The first type, exemplified by the New York statute, authorizes divorce when the parties have lived apart for the specified time pursuant to a separation decree. Thus either party may obtain the divorce under this form of the statute, regardless of how the separation came about so long as it exists pursuant to a decree. Fault is completely irrelevant.

The second type of statute authorizes the divorce when the parties have, for the statutory period, lived apart "voluntarily" or "willingly." A Maryland case construes this type of statute to impose three requirements for divorce: (a) An express or implied mutual agreement to separate, accompanied by a mutual intent not to resume the relationship. (b) For the prescribed period the parties must voluntarily have lived apart without cohabitation. (c) There is no reasonable hope of reconciliation.

The third class of statutes merely provides that the divorce may be granted when the parties have lived apart for the prescribed period of time. This should mean that fault is irrelevant and that either party may obtain the divorce no matter how the separation came about. This is what most of the cases hold.

5. Incompatibility

Five states recognize incompatibility as a ground for divorce (Alabama, Alaska, Delaware, New Mexico, and Oklahoma). Those of Alaska, New Mexico, and Oklahoma merely refer to incompatibility or incompatibility of temperament. The Alabama code refers to "such complete incompatibility that the parties can no longer live together." And the Delaware statute contains a redundant definition of incompatibility, authorizing divorce "when husband and wife are incompatible in that their marriage is characterized by rift or discord produced by reciprocal conflict of personalities existing for 2 consecutive years prior to the filing of the divorce action, and which has destroyed their relationship as husband and wife and the reasonable possibility of reconciliation."

Most definitions of incompatibility suggest that a marital relationship is incompatible when the parties can no longer live in harmony, when their interests and desires are seriously and irreconcilably at odds.

5. Miscellaneous Grounds for Divorce

There are several other grounds for divorce scattered through the statutes of the various states, none of them statistically important. These are indicated in the table which appears at the end of this chapter.

6. No-Fault or Marriage Breakdown

As a result of reform movements in the 1960's, and of the drafting of the Uniform Marriage and Divorce Act, fifteen states have adopted some version of marriage breakdown as a ground for divorce. These states are: Arizona, California, Florida, Hawaii, Idaho, Iowa, Kentucky, Michigan, Montana, Nebraska, New Hampshire, North Dakota, Oregon, and Texas. The Uniform Act sections are 303(2) and 305.

California was the first state to adopt this ground for divorce. Its statute and that of Oregon authorize dissolution of marriage when irreconcilable differences have caused the irremediable breakdown of the marriage. New Hampshire and North Dakota have similar provisions. The Iowa and Michigan statutes authorize dissolution of marriage when there has been a breakdown of marriage to such an extent that the legitimate objects of marriage have been destroyed and there remains no reasonable likelihood that the marriage can be preserved. The Florida statute just speaks in terms of irretrievable breakdown of marriage, expressly stating that that has occurred when neither of the parties denies the allegation of breakdown, and there are no minor children, but apparently leaving it to the trial court to determine without further standards when there are minor children or when one party denies that the marriage has broken down. There is provision for counseling or delay in the suit. Idaho authorizes the divorce for irreconcilable differences, defining

29

them (as do California and North Dakota) as those grounds which are determined by the court to be substantial reasons for not continuing the marriage and which make it appear that the marriage should be dissolved. In Texas the statute permits divorce without regard to fault if the marriage is unsupportable because of discord or conflict of personalities that destroys the legitimate ends of marriage and prevents any reasonable expectations of reconciliation. Finally, Colorado adopts verbatim the language of the Uniform Act, which authorizes divorce for irretrievable breakdown of the marriage, without defining that term further.

The meaning of the language used in all these statutes is not clear, since the terms are new to divorce law and there has not yet been time for extensive judicial interpretation. Therefore, the reader must turn to his or her attorney for the most current construction of the statutes if they reside in jurisdictions which have no-fault divorce laws.

Chapter VII

OUT-OF-STATE AND FOREIGN DIVORCES

Any divorce obtained in a state other than the state in which the parties are litigating or in which they reside, is termed a "foreign divorce" even though obtained not in a foreign country, but in a state other than the state of residence of the parties or in the state in which they are engaged in litigation.

Strictly speaking, foreign divorces may be divided into two categories--those granted by another state and those granted by another country. The state or country granting the divorce is known as the "rendering state." If a husband and wife were married in California and were then divorced by a California Court and thereafter moved to New York and engaged in litigation in New York, New York would regard the California divorce as a "foreign divorce" entitled to full faith and credit by virtue of the United States Constitution. On the other hand, if the husband and wife were married in State X and, having fallen upon unhappy days, separated with the wife moving to State Y and instituting a divorce action, thereupon returning immediately after obtaining her divorce to State X, the recognition of State Y's divorce judgment by State X would depend upon the following circumstances:

1. Did the wife establish a legal residence in State Y in accordance with the laws of State Y?

2. Was the husband personally served with a summons in State Y or did he appear personally in Court for the trial or by an attorney?

3. Did the wife comply with all of the requirements of State Y?

If both parties submitted to the jurisdiction of State Y and the Court in State Y found that the plaintiff had established a bona fide domicile in State Y, State X will be required to recognize the judgment of State Y.

If both parties were before the Court of State Y and a divorce was granted, the defeated spouse may not claim in subsequent litigation or in a subsequent law suit in State X or in State Z that the divorce granted by State Y was invalid or granted erroneously.

However, if a spouse has left his or her mate and has set up residence in another state and has then sued for a divorce after complying with the residence requirements of the state of new residence, the divorce, on its face, will be entitled to full faith and credit even if the wife did not appear to contest the suit. However, if the spouse who received the divorce then returns to the state of original residence, the other spouse may then challenge the divorce only to the extent of attacking the jurisdiction of the rendering states as fraudulent. The spouse against whom the divorce was granted may challenge the jurisdiction of the rendering state, since the question of jurisdiction was not litigated between the parties, if the spouse who was divorced did not appear in Court and either did not have an opportunity or, not having been served personally within the rendering state, did not choose to litigate the matter.

Divisible Divorces

The United States Supreme Court has held that there is such a judgment as a "divisible divorce." If a husband has abandoned his wife and has gone to another state and has obtained a divorce after living in the rendering state for a period equal to or in excess of the minimum residence requirement for filing an action for a divorce, he may obtain a divorce which is valid to terminate the marriage relationship and which will leave him free to remarry, but which will not necessarily extinguish his obligation to support his wife. He may have attained what the United States Supreme Court has described as a "divisible divorce" valid for purposes of terminating the marriage relationship, but not for purposes of terminating the husband's obligations to support the wife and the wife's right to receive support from the husband.

Some states even have statutes recognizing the doctrine of "divisible divorce." In New York State the statute is now known as the "Vanderbilt Law," since the case of Vanderbilt v. Vanderbilt which was carried from the Court of Appeals of the State of New York to the United States Supreme Court tested the validity of a New York statute which permitted the divorce to stand for purposes of terminating the marriage and barring the wife's right

32

to a separation or divorce, but did not permit the divorce to eliminate the rights of the wife, granted to her under the statute, to be awarded support notwithstanding the entry of the judgment of divorce, where the wife had not been served personally in the rendering state. A requirement of the statute is that the wife must have been a resident for one year before bringing her action.

This area of "divisible divorce" is one in which no layman should attempt to act without the advice of a lawyer. Proper action may require advice and knowledge and some study of the laws of two or more states--the state of original residence and the law of the rendering state.

There are instances in which a divorce may be attacked even though both parties appear. The attack may be a "direct attack" by a party to the divorce action or it may be a "collateral attack" by some third party who was not before the Court which rendered the divorce judgment. Such a third party may be a subsequent spouse of one of the parties to the original divorce. If the rendering state permits an attack on the divorce decree, either by one of the original parties or by a third party, the state of original residence will probably permit such an attack.

If the divorce is to be airtight, and if it is to withstand subsequent attacks, the residence in the rendering state must be bona fide and must not be a mere token compliance. Curbstone advice that you may rent a motel room or a one-room apartment and then be absent from the rendering state until the date of the trial, holding down your job in the state of your original residence, may be very costly. Not only will the rendering state inquire scrupulously as to the good faith and validity of your newly-acquired residence (Florida's outstanding judges are particularly strict and may impose severe penalties for misstatements or attempts to mislead the Court), but the judgment may be subject to attack in the state of original residence, not only to the obligations to pay alimony, but also with respect to the rights on inheritance and to the determination of status and the severance of the marriage relationship.

As a general rule, lawyers will advise clients who move to other states for the purpose of attaining a divorce to remain at least double the minimum time requirement before filing for divorce and to remain in the rendering state for the same period of time after the divorce has been granted.

This is another of the situations where each case may turn

33

upon its own peculiar fact. You should be guided by the advice of your attorney, and you should retain an attorney who is willing and able to cooperate with your attorney in the state of your original residence, unless you have no intention of ever returning to that state.

In the consideration of any foreign divorce decree or judgment, that is, any divorce granted in the state other than the state in which you reside, the questions which may arise are those of (1) status, that is the determination of the marriage bond for purposes of remarriage, (2) support and alimony, and (3) the question of rights and inheritance.

Insofar as custody of children is concerned, the children must be present in the State rendering the judgment for the custody judgment or decree to be effective and binding as an adjudication. The Court must have jurisdiction of both the subject of the action and of the person of the children.

The United States Supreme Court has rendered decisions on these questions which occasionally have reversed earlier decisions. Even in these opinions, and in these decisions made by the justices of the Court, presumably the nine best attorneys in the country, there have been disagreements, sometimes by margins of five to four, as to just what the law is or should be. Consequently, you should not attempt to use any self-help or advice in situations involving foreign divorces, but you should consult with your attorney and follow scrupulously the advice which he gives you.

Mexican Divorces

In states which require an extensive degree of proof, or in states which do not recognize mere physical separation, or incompatability of temperament as grounds for a divorce, many husbands and wives resort to the courts of the various states of the Republic of Mexico.

This again is an extremely sensitive area, with a number of states refusing to grant recognition to Mexican divorce judgments, even where there has been a substantial period of residence. Before travelling to Mexico, you should consult an attorney not only in the state of your present residence but in any state in which you plan to remarry or to reside.

34

While the Court of Appeals, the highest court in the State of New York, has recently recognized as valid judgments of divorce granted by courts of the states of the Republic of Mexico, where one spouse was physically present in Court and where the other spouse appeared by a duly authorized attorney, there are some states which do not follow this rule and which look with great disfavor not only upon parties, but also upon attorneys who participate in Mexican divorces. As a general rule, however, if the law of the forum or rendering state is satisfied by a minimum residence period and the opposing party has appeared and has litigated the matter or has stated in Court the lack of a desire to litigate the matter, the divorce thereafter rendered will be sustained.

The laws of most states of the Republic of Mexico recognize incompatability of temperament as a ground for divorce. This permits the award of a judgment of divorce without the stigma of misconduct which may be attached to divorces granted on the grounds of adultery, intolerable cruelty, assault or drunkenness.

Among the advantages of Mexican judgments of divorce are the lack of publicity in newspapers or other media, the ability to obtai n a divorce on innocuous grounds not stigmatizing either spouse and not embarrassing the children of the spouses, and the speed or expedition with which they may be granted. In these days of efficient air transportation, it is possible for a spouse, armed with a separation agreement and a power of attorney executed by the other spouse, to leave an Eastern city such as New York, Philadelphia or Washington in the morning, to arrive in El Paso, Texas, or in Juarez, Mexico, across the Rio Grande from El Paso, in the late afternoon or early evening, to appear in Court in Juarez on the following morning, and to leave during the afternoon with all proceedings completed, in time to return to work in the home city the following morning. Since there are two sets of attorneys' fees to be paid, however, those of the Mexican attorneys and those of the home state, Mexican divorces are usually a little more expensive, although considering the loss of time and the expense of drawn-out litigation, they are probably less expensive in the long run.

A disadvantage of a Mexican decree, however, may be a difficulty in enforcement in the home state, and hasty action, which may result in a divorce which upon reflection was not really desired or was not really to the advantage of either or both of the spouses or their children.

Chapter VIII
REMARRIAGE

No divorced person may remarry until his or her divorce decree becomes final.

The time within which a divorce decree becomes final will vary from state to state. In some states, such as California, it is as long as a year, while in other states the decree becomes final immediately and there are no restrictions upon remarriage.

Even where the decree becomes final, however, it may contain a provision prohibiting remarriage of either party for a stated period of time. Restrictions against remarriage usually do not apply to remarriage between the divorced spouses, who are permitted and in some states encouraged to remarry each other at any time. Ordinarily, their resumption of cohabitation as husband and wife during the period of the entry of the interlocutory decree and the final decree operates as a revocation of the interlocutory decree. In this connection, however, many circumstances and facts must be taken into account, and you should consult your lawyer before relying on any automatic provisions. The language of the statute may have been modified by a decision of a Court, or it may be subject to interpretation and may not be clear to a layman.

Different states have different rules. For example, in the State of Kentucky, not more than one divorce will be granted to a person except for adultery, or for clauses allowable to both a husband and wife, and remarriage in that State may become dangerous.

A person is not divorced until the divorce decree has become final, and any remarriage performed before the entry of a final divorce decree is void. However, once the divorce decree has become final, restrictions are imposed by some states and a remarriage within the prohibited period within the state may not only render the marriage void but may also subject the spouse marrying to a criminal or civil penalty.

In some states, remarriage within the prohibited period, even after the granting of the final decree, is punishable as bigamy.

The Table below indicates the restrictions on parties following divorce decrees.

REMARRIAGE OF DIVORCED SPOUSES

1. States in which there are no restrictions on remarriage:

ALASKA	IDAHO	NEW HAMPSHIRE
ARKANSAS	ILLINOIS	NEW JERSEY
CALIFORNIA	KENTUCKY	NEW MEXICO
COLORADO	MAINE	NORTH CAROLINA
CONNECTICUT	MARYLAND	OHIO
DELAWARE	MISSOURI	RHODE ISLAND
DISTRICT OF	MONTANA	SOUTH CAROLINA
COLUMBIA	NEBRASKA	WASHINGTON
FLORIDA	NEVADA	WYOMING
	HAWAII	

2. Restrictions on remarriage regulated by the Court:

GEORGIA--Judge or jury decides on restrictions, if any.

IOWA--One year restriction unless the Court consents to earlier marriage.

LOUISIAIA--Remarriage regulated by the Court, except that wife may not remarry for ten months after decree and where divorce is granted by reason of adultery, the guilty party may never marry the corespondent.

MICHIGAN--Restrictions, if any, provided in decree.

MISSISSIPPI--Court may prohibit guilty party from re-marrying.

NEW YORK--Guilty party may not remarry for three years,

38

and then only with permission of the Court.

NORTH DAKOTA--No remarriage allowed by either party unless the Court decree contains provisions permitting remarriage.

UTAH--No remarriage unless no appeal is taken, if no remarriage during pendency of appeal.

VERMONT--Remarriage regulated by Court, but no permission will be granted for two years, unless the former spouse is dead.

3. Remarriage prohibited for fixed period of time:

ALABAMA--Six days except that spouses may remarry.
ARIZONA--One year.
INDIANA--Two years if divorce obtained on default or by service by publication. If personal service and appearance by defendant, no restrictions.
KANSAS--Six months.
MASSACHUSETTS--Two years*.
MINNESOTA--Six months.
OKLAHOMA--Six months.
OREGON--Six months.
TEXAS--One year.
VIRGINIA--Four months restriction against either party, six months restriction against defendant guilty of adultery.
WEST VIRGINIA--60 days.
WISCONSIN--One year.
PUERTO RICO--No restrictions on husband, 301-day restriction on wife.
VIRGIN ISLANDS--30 days.

4. Restrictions against guilty parties:

MASSACHUSETTS--Two years.
NEW YORK--Three years, and then only by Court permission.

*MASSACHUSETTS, innocent party may remarry any time, guilty party prohibited from remarrying for two years.

4. Restrictions against guilty party (continued):

   LOUISIANA--Party guilty of adultery may never marry corespondent.
   PENNSYLVANIA--Party guilty of adultery may never marry corespondent during lifetime of innocent party.
   SOUTH DAKOTA--Where grounds are adultery, remarriage of guilty party prohibited during lifetime of innocent party.
   TENNESSEE--Party guilty of adultery may not remarry during lifetime of innocent party.

Chapter IX

ALIMONY AND PROPERTY RIGHTS

In all except a few states and territories of the United States, a wife who is successful in an action for a divorce or a separation is allowed "alimony" and in most states her Court costs and counsel fees as well. For a long period of time a wife who was granted an annulment received no alimony on the theory that the marriage, having been voided, never existed, whether it had been void from the beginning or merely voidable at the option or election of the injured or defrauded spouse. In recent years, however, many states have begun to allow the award of alimony to a wife whose marriage has been annulled provided she acted in good faith and otherwise was in a meritorious position. If, for example, a wife married her husband, believing that he was free to marry, whereas, in fact, a prior divorce obtained by the husband was invalid, the wife may be awarded alimony even though her marriage was void from the start since the husband had an existing marriage in effect at the time he and the wife participated in their ceremony of marriage.

The word "alimony" is derived from the Latin "alimonia," meaning sustenance. "Alimony" therefore is the sustenance, maintenance or support which the wife receives from her divorced husband. It stems from the common law right of the wife to be supported by her husband and to be nourished or sustained by him.

In the majority of states, there is legislation and there are statutes in effect giving the Court discretion to make an allowance for the support of the wife and the children not only permanently and in the judgment of divorce but "pendente lite," or during the pendency and carrying on of the law suit. This allowance is made not only to permit the wife to maintain the action if she has a reasonable ground or reasonable chance of succeeding, but also to keep her and the children from becoming public charges. In a few states, the husband, if disabled or necessitous, is allowed alimony from the priperty or earnings of the wife, but such instances are comparatively rare, and as a rule are limited to cases where if the wife does not furnish some support for the husband, he is likely to become a public charge, or to cases where the wife's income and assets were derived from the husband or as a result of the husband's efforts.

While the word "alimony," strictly speaking, refers only to support or sustenance for the wife, it is generally used to include both payments for the benefit of the wife which, strictly speaking, are "alimony" and payments for the benefit of the children which are known colloquially as "child support." Some judgments of divorce provide for the payment of "alimony" for the support of the wife and the minor children, while others provide for one periodic payment for the wife, to be made weekly or monthly, and another payment for the children. The allocation of the total amount of support to be paid to the wife is quite important, since the husband is allowed a tax deduction on monies paid solely for the support of the wife, while the wife must pay the tax on that sum. However, if there is a separate sum to be paid for the support of the children, the husband is required to pay the income tax on that amount, and the wife receives it tax-free albeit for the benefit of the children. Under some circumstances, it is possible for the parties, if they agree upon the requirements of the wife and the children, to allocate the payments to be paid to the wife between "alimony" and "child support," to lessen the tax impace by splitting the burden of the income tax and thus leaving more money available for support and less to be paid in taxes.

Alimony after a trial and in the final judgment is known as merely "alimony" or as "permanent alimony." Alimony awarded after the action has been started, but before it has been tried, is known variously as an "allowance," "temporary allowance," "temporary alimony," "alimony pendente lite," or "allowance pending trial." Alimony after the trial is generally referred to as "alimony" or "permanent alimony."

There are some states where no alimony is allowed on the theory that once a marriage is dissolved it is dissolved for all purposes. Notable among these states are Texas and Pennsylvania. Alimony is largely discretionary, and the exercise of judicial discretion may at times surprise laymen who merely rely on the words of the statute. As a rule, the Courts take into consideration all of the factors involved, including the husband's salary, the husband's earning ability, if he is not living up to his potentiality, or if he is obviously keeping his income low for alimony purposes, the amount of his capital, the amount of the wife's earning ability, the obligations of the wife to care for the children, which may leave her no time or no opportunity for gainful employment, the wife's earning ability and the wife's assets.

Until a few years ago, the law in many states provided for the husband to support the wife in accordance with the husband's means and earning ability honestly exercised, whether the wife happened to be a millionaire or a pauper. In recent years, however, Courts have taken a more realistic view, and the present tendency is for the Court to take into consideration the monies and capital available to the wife.

Also important and considered by the Courts is the standard of living to which the parties were accustomed and their station in life. If the parties lived beyond their means and if they maintained their standard of living only by a continuous invasion of capital, the Court trying the case or hearing the testimony of the parties may, in its discretion, direct that alimony be paid only out of income and without regard to the capital assets involved.

While the Courts in community property states are empowered to make divisions of community property, they usually do so without compelling either party to lost title to his or her separate property. Some states permit a Court to award to one spouse some portion of the capital assets of the other spouse, but these states are in the minority. The circumstances of the particular case may be controlling and you are warned to consult your attorney with respect to any difficult questions and to make a full disclosure to your attorney of your means and assets.

In some states, the Court may award the wife a lump sum in lieu of periodic and installment payments which otherwise might be directed. The Court may even invade the capital of the husband to have him pay certain bills and charges, particularly medical expenses incurred or to be incurred by an ill or needy wife or children or to pay educational expenses. In almost all states, the Courts have the power to regulate the occupancy of jointly-owned real property and in some states have the right and power to direct a transfer of title. In some instances the Court in a final judgment of divorce may restore to each party all property not otherwise disposed of which either party acquired from the other party during marriage.

As a general rule, where the husband sues his wife for a divorce and obtains a divorce, the wife does not receive permanent alimony although Courts have wide discretion in this regard. In some cases the Courts may even direct a wife who is divorced for her own misconduct to pay alimony to a husband and, in "balancing the equities and in taking into consideration the length of time the marriage has lasted, the conduct of the parties over a period of years, the number of children born of the marriage, and the means of both parties, as well as the station in life of the parties and the standard of living to which the parties and the children have become accustomed."

Where a husband sues his wife for divorce and obtains a judgment of divorce, the wife as a rule does not receive permanent alimony. In any event, however, if she shows a necessity for support pending the trial, she usually is allowed temporary alimony, and where the husband institutes the action, the wife is almost always allowed counsel fees. In most instances the counsel fees of the wife are charged to the husband, and he may be directed by the Court either in a temporary order or in the final judgment of divorce or separation or even in the judgment of annulment to pay counsel fees for the wife.

Where separation agreements are worked out, the counsel fees are subject to agreement by the parties and the attorneys. As a rule, the parties follow the prevailing law as enunciated by the Courts in contested matrimony cases, and both the amount of counsel fees and their incidence and the determination of the spouse who pays them are computed in accordance with the money available to both parties.

Chapter X

ENFORCEMENT AND MODIFICATION OF ALIMONY AWARDS

A judgment or decree which makes an award of alimony may be enforced by one or more proceedings. While the most commonly-encountered enforcement procedure is a motion or application to the Court which granted the judgment to punish the offending husband (or in the rare cases where a wife is directed to pay alimony or support or where the wife refuses to permit the husband to see the children, the offending wife) for contempt of Court for failure to comply with the judgment. "Contempt" is a most drastic remedy, and as a rule will be invoked only if the decree awarding the alimony cannot be enforced either by sequestration (seiquire of the defendant's property), or by reduction of the provisions of the decree to a money judgment and execution by the sheriff or marshall against the husband's property.

Money Judgment

If the spouse (usually the husband) who has been directed to pay alimony has not complied with the divorce decree, it may be easier and less costly for the wife to ask the Court to give her a money judgment against the husband. This money judgment may then be "docketed" or filed not only in the county in which the divorce was granted, but in any county in the State. It then becomes a "lien" on any real peoperty or real estate owned by the defendant, and the property cannot be sold without satisfying the lien. Where the husband has left the State but owns real property in the State, this is most effective. Likewise, if he maintains a bank account, business, or owns stocks or bonds which are held by a bank or custodial or which are in the temporary possession or custory of the wife, the money judgment will permit the sheriff or marshall to levy on the property and to satisfy the arrears out of the property. The real property of the defendant may likewise be sold at auction by the sheriff and the judgment satisfied from the proceeds.

Garnishee

In the usual case of a judgment, a garnishee of the defendant or debtor's earnings or income is permitted only up to ten percent of his property. Since a man earning $100.00 a week and directed to pay $40.00 a week alimony would pay only $10.00 a week, as opposed to $40.00, a garnishee in and of itself would not be particularly effective. However, the tendency has been to permit the Court to make an order on notice to the defendant's employer ordering the employer to deduct from the defendant's wages the amount of alimony and to forward this alimony directly to the wife. This in effect relieves the wife of the necessity of running after the husband, and as long as he is steadily employed and does not lose his job the judgment will be effective. In some cases, however, the entry of such an order may result in the defendant being discharged, and a wife should exercise supreme caution before taking this step.

Sequestration

If a husband cannot be found or if he can be found but refuses to make payment and the wife does not want to have him jailed for contempt of court, an alternative method is the "sequestration" of his property. In most states, an application to punish for contempt will not be entertained or heard by the Court unless the wife can swear that sequestration of property would have no effect or that the property has been so hidden and secreted that it cannot be located.

In the usual case of sequestration, if the husband has income-producing property, stocks, bonds, an automobile, jewelry and bank accounts, the wife may apply to the Court for the appointment of a receiver. Sometimes she herself will be appointed the receiver while on other occasions the Court will appoint some unbiased and disinterested third party. The receiver, when ap-

46

pointed, must file a bond to insure his faithful compliance with his duties. He is then empowered to seize the property and from the proceeds of the property, to pay the wife the amount which is due to her for her support and the support of the children.

The receiver is paid a percentage of the amount which he receives and pays out and he is held strictly accountable.

In some cases, where the delivery of the property to the receiver is resisted, the receiver may be required to retain an attorney to enforce his position as receiver.

This adds to the expense and leaves less money available for the wife and less money available for return to the husband in the event of the satisfaction of the wife's claim without the exhaustion of the fund or property seized by or delivered to the receiver.

Security for Future Payment

Where the husband has hidden his property or where he has no visible property but there has been no change in his circumstances in the time which has elapsed after the entry of the judgment directing the payment of the alimony, the Court may order him to show why he should not be punished for contempt of Court. If the Court finds that he is capable of making the payments and that he has not suffered any reverses or losses since the date of the hearing at which the alimony was fixed, he will be adjudged in contempt of Court and will be fined the amount of his arrears and he is directed to pay the fine, sometimes in weekly installments in addition to current alimony and sometimes in one lump sum or four or five lump sums over a period of time. As a rule, additional attorney's fees will be awarded to the wife and the husband in addition to being required to pay the amount of alimony, will also be required to pay more fees to the wife's attorneys.

When the husband is found guilty of contempt of Court, the order punishing him for contempt usually provides that if he does not make the payment directed in the finding order he may be arrested and placed in jail. The usual jail sentence is three months for payments under $500.00 and six months for payments of over $500.00. The sentences vary, however, and these terms are by

47

no means universal.

While contempt is a drastic remedy and as a rule will not be imposed unless there has been a clear showing of willful conduct as opposed to mere inability to pay, the wife should be cautious about asking for such relief. While the husband is in jail, his payments will be suspended for the period of his incarceration and need not be made up after his release. The wife, by putting her husband or former husband in jail, may in effect be "killing the goose that lays the golden egg." She may be better advised to enter a money judgment and to get as much as she can, in the meantime waiting for the husband's fortunes to improve on the theory that half a loaf is better than none.

If a husband has disposed of his property or if at the time of the trial he had stocks and bonds worth $10,000.00 but three months later has none, he must offer a satisfactory explanation of his reverses. By the same theory, if the husband has quit his job and cannot show a medical necessity for ceasing his employment, the Court will presume that he has done so without any adequate justification and the husband may be held guilty of contempt of Court. As a rule, a husband will be directed to pay alimony and child support in accordance with his means and with his earning ability honestly exercised. A man capable of earning $150.00 a week who takes a job at $50.00 a week may nevertheless be directed to pay $75.00 a week alimony if the Court finds that he willfully and without a valid reason rejected employment permitting him to make more money. The same applies to a husband who for no apparent reason decides to stop work and to take life a little easier. The Court may compel him either to work at an adequate salary if a position is obtainable or will incarcerate him if he does not work and does not attempt to obtain employment commeasurate with his ability.

In almost every case, it becomes a question of the husband's good faith and the Court will usually hold a hearing. In some states, such as New York, husbands may be jailed without a hearing, but the general tendency is against any such incarceration without an actual trial or hearing of live witnesses as opposed to a determination on papers.

48

Alimony Jails

In almost all states, a husband who has been guilty of willful defaults and who has been held in contempt of court will be placed in alimony jail. In some states he is placed in the County Jail while in other states there is a civil jail, as distinguished from a criminal jail, where he is confined, but is not confined at hard labor. However, in the words of an elderly publisher whose young third wife succeeded in having him committed to jail, "While the warden treated me well, jail is still jail."

Modification of Alimony Awards

If the husband loses his job, or if he suffers reverses and illness which decrease his earning potential, he may apply to the Court for a modification, reduction or postponement of the amounts of payments directed by the decree. He may make this application at any time there is a substantial change in his circumstances.

By the same token, if the needs of the wife and children increase by reason of accident, illness or because the children grow older and require more money, the wife may ask the Court to increase the amount. If the husband's circumstances improve and he earns more money, the wife may ask that she and the children be permitted to share in his affluence to improve their own standard of living. Typical examples of circumstances permitting increase are serious illness or accident suffered by one of the children requiring special care, illness or disability of the wife or of one of the children interfering with the wife making a living, or the inheritance by the husband of a large sum of money or his obtaining a new position at a vastly increased income.

Chapter XI

MARRIAGES AND RIGHTS OF MILITARY PERSONNEL

Throughout American military history, wartime marriages and peacetime marriages of persons serving in the Armed Forces have created problems peculiar to their status. As a general rule, marriages of military personnel are in the same category as marriages of members of the civilian community. Occasionally both husband and wife are members of the Armed Forces, and they may then find themselves subject to peculiar regulations either expanding or limiting not only their marital rights but their rights to pay and allowances. For example, if two members of the military establishment contract marriage and each person as a single or unmarried person was entitled to a quarters allowance, the quarters allowance may be reduced as a result of their marriage and limited to the allowance of a married person rather than to the two separate allowances.

Particularly since 1940, when Selective Service went into effect, many diverse questions have been asked of Military Legal Assistance Officers, Legal Aid Societies, Bar Associations and government officials as well as commanding officers about the marital status of literally millions of enlisted and commissioned members of the Armed Forces and their dependents.

When there is a State of War or a State of Emergency, almost all States provide for waivers of waiting periods prior to the performance of marriage. In substantially all jurisdictions the medical certificate of an officer of the Armed Forces will be accepted by the licensing authority.

In almost all commands outside the limits of the continental United States and in many commands within the continental United States, it is necessary for a member of the Armed Forces to obtain the permission of his commanding officer before contracting a marriage. This permission may be required even if the marriage is to be performed in the United States if the serviceman or servicewoman is stationed outside the United States and is to return to that station after the expiration of a period of leave or furlough or temporary assignment.

If you are in the military service and are contracting marriage, you should make an inquiry of the Adjutant of your unit or to the Staff Judge Advocate or Legal Assistance Officer. The Legal Assistance Officer will be in a position to advise you of the local licensing requirements and to assist you in obtaining the necessary documents, including your medical certificate. It is important that you familiarize yourself with the requirements, since there are a few jurisdictions where officials or even clergymen will be reluctant to perform marriage ceremonies if they feel that by performing such ceremonies they may jeopardize the serviceman's or servicewoman's standing in the Armed Forces.

While the validity of the marriage of a person in military service probably will not be affected adversely by a marriage without permission of the proper military authorities, the person participating in such a marriage may subject himself to punishment under Article 15 of the Uniform Code of Military Justice or even to trial by Court Martial. The Army, Navy, and Air Force regulations covering marriages of military personnel are promulgated not only to promote the greater efficiency of the Armed Forces, but also to protect members of the military establishment against hasty and ill-advised marriages and to protect them from precipitous action which they may regret and attempt to undo.

Persons in military service should keep in mind that in marrying they accept obligations not imposed upon them prior to marriage and that in some circumstances the performance of a marriage ceremony may bar the serviceman or servicewoman from promotion or from attendance at a Service school or from some other desirable military assignment. Since these regulations change from time to time, it is important that the person in military service be familiar with all factors involved, since postponement of the marriage may be mutually advantageous and may build a better foundation for the years ahead.

Residence as Affected by Military Service

Most States of the Union provide that a serviceman may not lose his residence by reason of military service. Some States provide that a residence may not be gained solely by reason of military service. If you should be stationed in a State whose marriage and divorce laws are more favorable to your particular situation than those of your home State and you desire to acquire a residence in the State in which you are stationed, you should not only obtain a new residence address within that State but you should effect a change on all of your service records indicating that your residence has been transferred. You should notify the Board of Elections of your home state, obtain an automobile operator's license in the State of new residence, transfer your bank accounts and take all other steps which you would take as a civilian to effect a permanent change of residence. Military service alone and assignment to a post, camp, station, base, or port in a new State will not be sufficient to effect a change of residence. The actual physical presence must be supplemented by the steps necessary to establish residence to the same effect as if you were a civilian.

Residence for Purposes of
Matrimonial Actions

The rules governing residence for purposes of matrimonial actions may vary with your status in the action, whether plaintiff or defendant. The tendency of the courts is to afford ample protection to a person in military service and if you are a plaintiff in military service suing for a divorce, annulment, or separation, you will still be required to sustain the burden of showing the establishment of a new residence. On the other hand, if you are a defendant the burden on your spouse who is bringing the action will be considerably heavier since you will be afforded the protections not only of the Soldiers and Sailors Civil Relief Act of 1940 as amended (a Congressional enactment protecting servicemen in all jurisdictions of the United States) but also the Soldiers and Sailors Civil Relief Act or Military Relief Act of the particular State. These acts vary, but they must afford at least the same protection given to service personnel by the Con-

52

gressional enactment.

If you are absent from your State while on military duty, it will be extremely difficult for your spouse to obtain a divorce unless you authorize an attorney to appear for you. A default judgment usually will not be permitted unless your rights are protected not only by actual notice to you but by the appointment of a lawyer delegated by the Court to protect your rights. If your testimony is necessary for the protection of your rights, the case may either be placed on the "military suspense calendar" until your return to the United States or your return to your particular State if your military assignment takes you to another jurisdiction within the United States and not in a foreign country, or by holding the case in abeyance until after you have had an opportunity to determine whether you want to defend the case and what steps you want to take to hire a lawyer to present testimony in your behalf.

Service of Process on
Military Personnel

Some military reservations within the United States are exclusively Federal--and process of State courts may not be served within the borders of the military reservation. Others are merely on land leased from the State or ceded by the State for a period of years, often with the express reservation to the State of the right to serve the process of its courts on the Federal reservation. Not only do the facts and the applicable rules of law differ from military reservation to military reservation, and often with the same State, but in some instances, particularly where there is a large military reservation, the right to serve State process is reserved to the State in some portions of the reservation and waived in other portions. If you do not want to be bothered with the action until the completion of emergency service you should confer immediately with the Staff Judge Advocate of your post, camp, station, base, or port and have him make an inquiry on your behalf to the Department of Defense, the Department of the Interior, Department of Justice or the particular State involved.

Caution

Be extremely careful about writing to the Court or a Judge or Clerk of Court after you have received process of either a summons or complaint. One of the criteria of the State in which the process has been issued may be whether you receive actual notice. If you received actual notice, you may be subject to a judgment of default or you may be required to file an answer or have an attorney, either privately retained or engaged by legal aid or a veteran's organization, appear for you.

Before you write any letters, consult the legal assistance officer of your unit and, if possible, consult an attorney in your home State or town.

Chapter XII

PROCEDURE FOR OBTAINING AN
ANNULMENT, SEPARATION OR DIVORCE

If you are married and feel that your marriage is damaged beyond repair or if you feel that there are legal obstacles which prevent your marriage from ever becoming valid, or if you feel that a mandatory period of separation is the only thing which can save your marriage, or if for personal or religious reasons you are opposed to a divorce or final termination of your marriage, your first step is to make up your own mind as to the course of conduct which will best promote the happiness or welfare of all concerned. You must think not only of yourself but also of your children and of the other people who may be affected by the continuance or by the dissolution or even by the suspension of your marriage.

Very few laymen are qualified to assess the legal validity of either a marriage or the strength of a case for its declaration of nullity, its suspension or its dissolution.

Your first step, therefore, after you have made your personal and emotional decision, is to consult a lawyer.

If you do not have a lawyer of your own, you may communicate with the local Bar Association--either the City or Town Bar Association, the County Bar Association or the State Bar Association. Almost all Bar Associations have what are known as "legal referral services," which will be glad to furnish to you without charge a lawyer having some familiarity with your particular type of problem. Most of these legal referral services will direct you to a lawyer who will agree to charge you a flat and extremely reasonable fee for a one-half hour consultation, but who will charge you at his usual rates for any conferences in excess of one-half hour. In this way you know that you will not waste the time of a lawyer who does not take or act in Family

Court matters, and you will not wast your own time by consulting a lawyer who will not under any circumstances accept your case. There are many lawyers who shy away from family or matrimonial litigation and there are many others who are not temperamentally equipped for what may be a rather tumultuous situation accompanied by turmoil and vindictiveness. Litigation between a husband and wife who were once in love or who are still in love can exceed in bitterness and hatred almost any other type of Court proceeding.

Preparing for Your Conference
With the Lawyer

After you have telephoned to the lawyer and have made an appointment, prepare a statement for him giving him the following information:

1. The date and place of your birth. (If you are contemplating an action for dissolution on the ground that you are not of legal age to consent to the marriage, you should have a copy of your birth or baptismal certificate with you.)

2. The date and place of the birth of your husband or wife.

3. The date and place of your marriage and the nature of the ceremony (civil or religious).

4. The date and place of any prior marriages contracted either by you or by your spouse, together with a statement of the date, place and circumstances (whether by death, disappearance, divorce or annulment) of each such marriage.

5. The name, date of birth and place of birth of each child born during the marriage or adopted during the marriage.

6. A short statement of why the lawyer is being consulted --whether merely to seek advicr on state of fact situations, to take action to declare the nullity of the marriage, to obtain a separation, or to obtain a divorce.

7. The income and assets, roughly stated, of both spouses.

If you have prepared this statement, there will be more time for you to ask the lawyer the questions, and he can read in a few moments facts which might consume ten or fifteen minutes of your interview if you were to sit by and answer his questions.

Do not attempt to draw any conclusions of law--that is why the lawyer studied for many years. If you feel that you can trust

56

the lawyer, you should tell him everything and should hold back nothing, dealing with him as if he were a clergyman or a physician. If you do not trust him, you should not consult him in the first place. If you have a family lawyer or a lawyer with whom you have dealt previously, you will, of course, have a certain amount of confidence in him before you consult him, and if he himself does not accept retainers in matrimonial or family law cases, he can refer you to someone in whom you can have the same condifence which you have reposed in him in the past.

Taking Action

Let us assume that for reasons which you accept, the marriage for all personal and emotional purposes is over. The lawyer will still discuss with you the possibility of reconciliation. If he can save a marriage which is worth saving, he will make an attempt to do so and you should not dismiss these attempts on his part as interference or as the well-meaning machinations of an impractical "do-gooder." In some states conciliation procedures are mandatory, while in other states local custom or canons of ethics require the lawyer to make an attempt to reconcile the parties.

Above all, follow your lawyer's advice. If he tells you to stay away from bars or to stay away from race tracks or dog tracks or to avoid the company of certain persons, by all means follow his advice. If you do not understand his advice or do not understand the reasons for it, ask him and he will give you an answer which is reasonable. He may explain to you that he is "playing a hunch" and you should keep in mind that his "hunch" is based upon study and experience.

However, if the decision is irrevocable, the lawyer will prepare a complaint (see appendix) based upon the facts which you have related to him and which his own investigation has disclosed, setting forth the facts and the relief which you ask the Court to grant, generally described as the "prayer for relief."

The prayer for relief will vary from state to state, since laws and procedure vary in the different American jurisdictions.

In some states, the complaint, accompanied by a summons, may be served on the defendant or the other spouse immediately while in other states is must first be filed in Court and may not

57

mencement of the law suit and the final hearing, either because some states require such a delay for "cooling off" or for mandatory conciliation procedures, or because the Court calendars are crowded, congested, or not up-to-date, some temporary arrangements may be made for custody. However, once the contested trial proceeds, evidence is presented and if there is a jury trial, the Judge will make the final decision and sign the judgment after the jury has returned its verdict. If there is a trial before a Judge alone without a jury or before a referee or special master, the Judge may sign the decision, either announcing his decision at the close of the trial or reserving his decision until he has made a further study of the law and the evidence. Where cases are tried before a "special master" or before a "referee" the special master or referee may make a recommendation to the Judge who will then act to review and either confirm or disaffirm the report and recommendations of the special master or referee.

After the evidence has been completed and after the judgment has been signed, it may be a final judgment or a form of judgment which is known as "interlocutory" which means that it will not become final for a stated period of time after its signature. In some states the judgment of divorce is fina, but there is a prohibition against remarriage, while in other states the judgment of divorce or annulment is interlocutory only and will not be a final judgment, leaving a spouse free to remarry or invalidating rights of inheritance, until a certain period of time has elapsed.

You should also consult your attorney and be sure that you understand what he tells you about interlocutory decrees and final decrees. In some states, the interlocutory decree becomes a final decree as a matter of course, while in other states a separate final decree must be entered.

In dealing with your attorney, keep in mind that your case is just as important to him as it is to you, but that yours is not the only case in his office. You should not call him every time some question arises in your mind, but should call him only at stated intervals. Try to call him only once on any particular day and wherever you have a particular question which seems troublesome drop him a note and tell him you will call him a day or two later, thus giving him a chance to investigate any questions of fact or of law which may be required for the answer to your question.

be served until after it has been filed or "noticed."

After service or delivery to the defendant-husband or wife, there is a mandatory period during which the defendant may answer either in person or by his or her attorney. If the defendant does not want to continue the marriage and does not desire to contest the case or if you yourself, as defendant, are served with a summons and complaint and do not desire to oppose the divorce, you may merely "default" and may fail to appear or answer, and the divorce will proceed by "inquest." A divorce, separation, or annulment is not something which may be had for the asking, but you must prove that the grounds exist. If your husband or wife denies that the grounds exist, he or she may then file an "answer" denying the charges made and a hearing which is conducted after service of an answer is known as a "trial." However, if the defendant spouse does not want to contest the action for a divorce, separation, or annulment, he or she may merely fail to answer and the hearing which is then held after the "default" is known as an "inquest" at which the only obligation is to satisfy the Court that a cause of action exists. At a "trial" as opposed to an "inquest" the plaintiff or the spouse who brings the suit or action must present a preponderance of the evidence establishing his or her right to relief--in non-legal language, the plaintiff or suing spouse must "have a better case." If the cases are equally balanced no divorce, separation, or annulment will be granted.

If there is no "appearance" or answer by the defendant and the time within which he or she is permitted to "appear" or "answer passes without any word, there is a default and the case may be set down for an uncontested hearing or inquest. At such a hearing, held before a Judge, a Court-appointed Referee, or a "special master," the plaintiff wil present his or her proof by way of documents and oral testimony, and if the trier of the facts is satisfied that a case has been made out for relief, a judgment will be granted on default.

If an answer is filed, there may be various pre-trial proceedings in the course of which applications for temporary or interim relief may be made. Temporary alimony may be awarded based upon a short hearing or upon affidavits and documentary proof, and partial or interim counsel fees may be awarded. At the same time, if there is likely to be a delay between the com-

59

FEES AND COSTS: Fees charged by lawyers vary considerably, both from State to State, County to County, from City to City, and from lawyer to lawyer. You should be prepared to pay some retainer fee to your lawyer, even in jurisdictions where the practice is for the husband to pay the fees of both lawyers. Clients have a way of becoming dissatisfied with lawyers, but experience has shown that they are less likely to become dissatisfied with lawyers in whom they have made an investment of money, just as the lawyer will become less dissatisfied with a client in whom he has made an investment of time which to him is money. Above all, avoid misunderstandings with your lawyer on the question of fees. He may not be able to give you a final fee, but you should be prepared to pay him from time to time so your bill does not mount up to a figure which to you may be astronomical, although it may be the standard charge in a case such as yours. Frankness and full discussion are recommended, and dealings on a cash basis with a final payment at the conclusion of the case are recommended. Extensive credit is unsatisfactory both to the lawyer and to the client and should be avoided. A lawyer will have much more enthusiasm for the case of a client who is frank and honorable with him.

Conclusion

This legal almanac does not purport to answer all or even a majority of your questions. The same is true for all of the legal almanac series. No legal almanac can take the place of your lawyer, but your reading a legal almanac prior to your consultation with the lawyer will make his work easier and will lead to a more satisfactory disposition of your case.

LEGAL AGE FOR MARRIAGE AND LICENSE REQUIREMENTS

State	Minimum Age F	Minimum Age M	Parental Consent Required if Below Age of: F	Parental Consent Required if Below Age of: M	Medical Required for License	Waiting Period Before License	Waiting Period After License
Alabama	14	17	18	21	yes	no	no
Alaska	16	18	18	19	yes	yes—3 days	no
Arizona	16	16	18	18	yes	no	no
Arkansas	16	17	18	21	yes	yes—3 days	no
California	16	18	18	21	yes	no	no
Colorado	16	16	18	18	yes	no	no
Connecticut	16	16	18	18	yes	yes—4 days	no
Delaware	16	18	18	18	yes	no	yes*
District of Columbia	16	18	18	21	yes	yes—3 days	no
Florida	16	18	21	21	yes	yes—3 days	no
Georgia	16	18	18	18	yes	yes—3 days	3 days if under age
Hawaii	16	17	18	18	yes	no	no
Idaho	16	16	18	18	yes	no	no
Illinois	16	—	18	18	yes	no	no

* 24 hours for residents; 96 hours for out-of-state residents

State	Minimum Age F	M	Parental Consent Required if Below Age of: F	M	Medical Required for License	Waiting Period Before License	Waiting Period After License
Indiana	17	17	18	18	yes	yes--3 days	no
Iowa	16	18	18	18	yes	yes--3 days	no
Kansas	18	18	18	18	yes	yes--3 days	no
Kentucky	16	18	18	18	yes	yes--3 days	no
Louisiana	16	18	18	18	yes	no	yes--72 hours
Maine	16	16	18	18	yes	yes--5 days	no
Maryland	16	18	18	21	no	yes--48 hours	no
Massachusetts	12	14	18	18	yes	yes--3 days	no
Michigan	16	—	18	18	yes	yes--3 days	no
Minnesota	16	18	18	18	no	yes--5 days	no
Mississippi	15	17	21	21	yes	yes--3 days	no
Missouri	15	15	18	21	yes	yes--3 days	no
Montana	16	18	18	21	yes	yes--5 days	no
Nebraska	16	18	19	19	yes	yes--5 days	no
Nevada	16	18	18	18	no	no	no
New Hampshire	13	14	18	18	yes	yes--5 days	no
New Jersey	16	16	18	18	yes	yes--72 hours	no
New York	14	16	18	21	yes	no	yes--24 hours
New Mexico	16	16	18	18	yes	no	no

State	Minimum Age F	Minimum Age M	Parental Consent Required if Below Age of: F	Parental Consent Required if Below Age of: M	Medical Required for License	Waiting Period Before License	Waiting Period After License
North Carolina	16	16	18	18	yes	no	no
North Dakota	15	18	18	18	yes	no	no
Ohio	16	18	18	18	yes	yes—5 days	no
Oklahoma	15	18	18	21	yes	no	no
Oregon	15	18	18	18	yes	yes—7 days	no
Pennsylvania	16	16	18	18	yes	yes—3 days	no
Puerto Rico	16	18	21	21	yes	no	no
Rhode Island	16	18	18	18	yes	yes—5 days	no
South Carolina	14	16	18	18	no	yes—24 hours	no
South Dakota	16	18	18	18	yes	no	no
Tennessee	16	16	18	18	yes	yes—3 days	no
Texas	16	16	18	18	yes	no	no
Utah	14	16	18	21	yes	no	yes—5 days
Vermont	16	18	18	18	yes	no	no
Virginia	16	18	18	18	yes	no	no
Washington	17	17	18	18	no	yes—3 days	no
West Virginia	16	18	18	18	yes	yes—3 days	no
Wisconsin	16	18	18	18	yes	yes—5 days	no
Wyoming	16	18	21	21	yes	no	no

APPENDIX B

Relationships within which a man (or woman within
corresponding degrees) is prohibited from marriage:
All States

> Grandmother
> Mother
> Daughter
> Granddaughter
> Aunt
> Niece
> Sister
> Half-sister

ALABAMA:

> Step-mother
> Step-daughter
> Wife's granddaughter
> Daughter-in-law

ALASKA:

> Grand-aunt
> First Cousin
> Grand-niece
> First Cousin once removed
> Second Cousin

ARIZONA:

> First Cousin

ARKANSAS:

> First Cousin

COLORADO:

> First Cousin

CONNECTICUT:

> Step-mother
> Step-daughter

DELAWARE:

> First Cousin

DISTRICT OF COLUMBIA: Step-mother
Step-daughter
Step-grandmother
Grandson's Wife
Mother-in-law
Wife's Grandmother
Wife's Granddaughter
Daughter-in-law

GEORGIA: Step-mother
Step-daughter
Mother-in-law
Grandmother
Daughter-in-law

IDAHO: First Cousin

ILLINOIS: First Cousin

INDIANA: Grand-aunt
First Cousin
Grand-niece
First Cousin once removed

IOWA: First Cousin
Step-mother
Step-daughter
Grandson's Wife
Mother-in-law
Daughter-in-law

KANSAS: First Cousin

KENTUCKY: First Cousin
Grand-niece
First Cousin once removed
Step-mother
Step-daughter

65

KENTUCKY: (continued)	Grandfather's Wife Grandson's Wife Mother-in-law Wife's Grandmother Wife's Granddaughter Daughter-in-law
LOUISIANA:	First Cousin
MAINE:	Step-mother Step-daughter Grandfather's Wife Grandson's Wife Mother-in-law Wife's Grandmother Wife's Granddaughter Daughter-in-law
MARYLAND:	Step-mother Step-daughter Grandfather's Wife Grandson's Wife Mother-in-law Wife's Grandmother Wife's Granddaughter Daughter-in-law
MASSACHUSETTS:	Step-mother Step-daughter Grandfather's Wife Grandson's Wife Mother-in-law Wife's Grandmother Wife's Granddaughter Daughter-in-law
MICHIGAN:	First Cousin Step-mother

66

MICHIGAN: Step-daughter
(continued)   Grandfather's Wife
                   Grandson's Wife
                   Mother-in-law
                   Wife's Grandmother
                   Wife's Granddaughter
                   Daughter-in-law

MINNESOTA: Grand Aunt
                   First Cousin
                   Grand Niece
                   First Cousin once removed

MISSISSIPPI: First Cousin
                   Step-mother
                   Step-daughter
                   Daughter-in-law

MISSOURI: First Cousin

MONTANA: First Cousin

NEBRASKA: First Cousin

NEVADA: First Cousin

NEW HAMPSHIRE: First Cousin
                   Step-mother
                   Step-daughter
                   Grandson's Wife
                   Mother-in-law
                   Daughter-in-law

NORTH CAROLINA: First Cousin
                   Double First Cousin

NORTH DAKOTA: First Cousin

OHIO: Grand-aunt
                               First Cousin
                               Grand-niece
                               First Cousin once removed

OKLAHOMA: First Cousin
                               First Cousin once removed
                               Second Cousin
                               Step-mother
                               Step-daughter

OREGON: Grand-aunt
                               Grand-niece
                               First Cousin

PENNSYLVANIA: First Cousin
                               Step-mother
                               Step-daughter
                               Wife's Granddaughter
                               Daughter-in-law

RHODE ISLAND: Step-mother
                               Step-daughter
                               Grandfather's Wife
                               Grandson's Wife
                               Mother-in-law
                               Wife's Grandmother
                               Wife's Granddaughter
                               Daughter-in-law

SOUTH CAROLINA: Step-mother
                               Step-daughter
                               Grandfather's Wife
                               Grandson's Wife
                               Mother-in-law
                               Wife's Grandmother
                               Wife's Granddaughter
                               Daughter-in-law

SOUTH DAKOTA:	First Cousin
	First Cousin once removed
	Step-mother
	Step-daughter
TENNESSEE:	Grand-niece
	Step-mother
	Grandfather's Wife
	Grandson's Wife
	Wife's Grandmother
	Wife's Granddaughter
	Daughter-in-law
TEXAS:	Step-mother
	Step-daughter
	Wife's Granddaughter
	Daughter-in-law
UTAH:	Grand-aunt
	Grand-niece
	First Cousin
VERMONT:	Step-mother
	Step-daughter
	Grandfather's Wife
	Grandson's Wife
	Mother-in-law
	Wife's Grandmother
	Wife's Granddaughter
	Daughter-in-law
VIRGINIA:	Step-mother
	Daughter-in-law
	Step-daughter
	Wife's Granddaughter
	Wife's Niece
WASHINGTON:	First Cousin

69

WASHINGTON: (continued)	First Cousin once removed
	Grand-aunt
	Grand-niece

WEST VIRGINIA: Step-mother
Daughter-in-law
Step-daughter
Wife's Granddaughter
Wife's Step-daughter
First Cousin
Double First Cousin
Wife or Widow of Brother's or
   Sister's Son

WISCONSIN: First Cousin (unless female is 55
   years old)
Double First Cousin
First Cousin once removed

WYOMING: First Cousin

PUERTO RICO: Adopted Daughter
First Cousin

VIRGIN ISLANDS: Firs. Cousin

70

MARRIAGES WHICH ARE PROHIBITED
ON RACIAL GROUNDS (PERSON OF
CAUCASIAN RACE AND OTHER RACE)

NEGRO:

Alabama
Arkansas
Delaware
Florida
Georgia
Idaho
Kentucky
Louisiana
Maryland
Mississippi
Missouri
North Carolina
Oklahoma
South Carolina
Tennessee
Texas
Virginia
West Virginia

ORIENTAL OR
MONGOLIAN:

Georgia
Louisiana
Maryland
Mississippi
Virginia

AMERICAN INDIAN:

Georgia
Louisiana
North Carolina
South Carolina
Virginia

These laws are now void and unenforcible.

71

APPENDIX C

STATUTORY REQUIREMENTS TO CREATE A VALID MARRIAGE

State	License Valid For	Medical Certificate Effective For	Minumum Waiting Period - - License Application To Ceremony	Minumum Waiting Period - - Medical Exam To Ceremony
ALABAMA	30 days	30 days	NONE	NONE
ALASKA	365 days	365 days	3 days*	3 days
ARIZONA	Indefinite	30 days	NONE	48 hours
ARKANSAS	Indefinite	30 days	3 days	3 days
CALIFORNIA	90 days	30 days	NONE	NONE
COLORADO	Indefinite	30 days	NONE	NONE
CONNECTICUT	60 days	40 days	4 days*	4 days
DELAWARE	30 days	30 days	24 hours*	24 hours*
DISTRICT OF COLUMBIA	Indefinite	NOT REQUIRED	4 days	NOT APPLICABLE
FLORIDA	30 days	30 days	3 days	3 days
GEORGIA	Indefinite	30 days	NONE	NONE
HAWAII	30 days	30 days	3 days	3 days
IDAHO	Indefinite	30 days	NONE	NONE
ILLINOIS	30 days	15 days	1 day	1 day
INDIANA	60 days	30 days	3 days	3 days

State	License Valid For	Medical Certificate Effective For	Minimum Waiting Period-- License Application To Ceremony	Minimum Waiting Period-- Medical Exam To Ceremony
IOWA	20 days	20 days	3 days	3 days
KANSAS	Indefinite	30 days	3 days*	3 days*
KENTUCKY	30 days	15 days	3 days	3 days
LOUISIANA	Indefinite	10 days	72 hours*	72 hours*
MAINE	1 year	30 days	5 days	5 days
MARYLAND	6 months	NOT REQUIRED	48 hours*	NOT APPLICABLE
MASS.	60 days	30 days	3 days*	3 days*
MICHIGAN	Indefinite	30 days	3 days*	3 days*
MINNESOTA	Indefinite	NOT REQUIRED	5 days*	NOT APPLICABLE
MISSISSIPPI	Indefinite	30 days	3 days	3 days
MISSOURI	10 days	15 days	3 days	3 days
MONTANA	Indefinite	20 days	5 days*	5 days*
NEBRASKA	Indefinite	30 days	NONE	NONE
NEVADA	Indefinite	NOT REQUIRED	NONE	NOT APPLICABLE
NEW HAMPSHIRE	90 days	30 days	5 days	5 days
NEW JERSEY	30 days	30 days	72 hours	72 hours
NEW MEXICO	Indefinite	30 days	NONE	NOT APPLICABLE
NEW YORK	60 days	30 days	24 hours	3 days

State	License Valid For	Medical Certificate Effective For	Minimum Waiting Period-- License Application To Ceremony	Minimum Waiting Period-- Medical Exam To Ceremony
NORTH CAROLINA	Indefinite	30 days	48 hours for non-residents	48 hours for non-residents
NORTH DAKOTA	60 days	30 days*	NONE	NONE
OHIO	60 days	30 days	5 days*	5 days*
OKLAHOMA	30 days	30 days	72 hours if other party a minor	72 hours if other party a minor
OREGON	Indefinite	30 days	7 days*	7 days*
PENNSYLVANIA	60 days	30 days	3 days	3 days
RHODE ISLAND	Indefinite	40 days	5 days for non-resident female*	5 days for non-resident female
SOUTH CAROLINA	Indefinite	NOT REQUIRED	24 hours	NOT APPLICABLE
SOUTH DAKOTA	20 days	20 days	NONE	NOT APPLICABLE
TENNESSEE	Indefinite	Certificate satisfactory to Clerk issuing decree	3 days*	3 days*
TEXAS	15 days	15 days	NONE	NONE
UTAH	Indefinite	30 days	NONE	NOT APPLICABLE

State	License Valid For	Medical Certificate Effective For	Minimum Waiting Period -- License Application To Ceremony	Minimum Waiting Period -- Medical Exam To Ceremony
VERMONT	Indefinite	30 days	5 days*	5 days*
VIRGINIA	60 days	30 days	NONE	NOT APPLICABLE
WASHINGTON	30 days		3 days	3 days
WEST VIRGINIA	Indefinite	30 days	3 days	
WISCONSIN	30 days	15 days	5 days	5 days
WYOMING	Indefinite	30 days	NONE	NOT APPLICABLE
PUERTO RICO	Indefinite	Certificate sufficient to licensing authority	NONE	NONE
VIRGIN ISLANDS	Indefinite	NOT REQUIRED	8 days*	NOT APPLICABLE

* May be waived by Court on sufficient showing of necessity or good reason
 (including military service or pregnancy)
 90 hours for non-residents
 3 days if parties are under 21, except where female is under 21 and signs
 an affidavit of pregnancy.
 Medical certificate may be waived if female is pregnant.

KANSAS: Neither authorized or prohibited and sometimes performed.

NEBRASKA: Permitted if both parties are members of a religious sect recognizing proxy marriage and if performed in accordance with rules of sect.

NEW MEXICO: Opinion by Attorney General upholding validity of proxy marriages but not recommended.

NEW YORK: Not explicitly authorized but not contrary to public policy if valid in state where contracted.

TEXAS: Permitted where one party in Military Service.

PUERTO RICO: Permitted by means of mandate through special power of attorney.

MONTANA: Permitted if formerly acknowledged before a Clerk of Court and 2 witnesses and filed with premarital certificate attached.

NEW YORK: Expressly authorized.

SOUTH CAROLINA: Recognized.

APPENDIX D
AGE OF CONSENT FOR MARRIAGE

| | Without Parent's Consent | | With Parent's Consent | |
	Males	Females	Males	Females
AL	21	18	17	14
AK	19	18	18	16 *
AZ	18	18	18	16 *
AR	21	18	17	16 *
CA	18	18	With parent's consent—parental consent alone is not sufficient; court approval is also required.	
CO	18	18	16	16 **
CT	18	18	16	16 *
DE	18	18	18	16 *
DC	21	18	18	16
FL	18	18	18	16 *
GA	18	18	18	16 *
HI	16	16	15	15
ID	18	18	16	16 **
IL	21	18	18	16 *
IN	18	18	17	17 *
IA	18	18	18	16 *
KS	18	18	14	12
KY	18	18	18	16 *
LA	18	18	18	16 **
ME	18	18	16	16 **
MD	18	18	16	16 *
MA	18	18	With parent's consent—parental consent alone is not sufficient; court approval is also required.	
MI	18	18	18	16 *
MN	18	18	18	16 **
MS	21	21	17	15 **

* There are provisions for waiver in case of pregnancy.
** Uner this age court approval is required.

77

	Without Parent's Consent		With Parent's Consent	
	Males	Females	Males	Females
MO	21	18	15	15 **
MT	18	18	With parents' consent-parental consent alone is not sufficient; court approval is also required.	
NE	19	19	18	16 *
NV	18	18	18	16 *
NH	18	18	With parents' consent-parental consent alone is not sufficient; court approval is also required.	
NJ	18	18	18	16 **
NM	18	18	16	16 *
NY	21	18	16	14 **
NC	18	18	16	16 *
ND	18	18	18	15
OH	21	21	18	16
OK	21	18	18	15 *
OR	18	18	18	15
PA	18	18	16	16 **
RI	18	18	18	16 *
SC	18	18	16	14 *
SD	18	18	18	16 *
TN	18	18	16	16
TX	18	18	16	16
UT	21	18	16	14
VT	18	18	18	16 **
VA	18	18	18	16
WA	18	18	17	17 **
WV	18	18	18	16 *
WI	18	18	16	16
WY	19	19	18	16

* There are provisions for waiver in case of pregnancy.
** Under this age court approval is required.

APPENDIX E
SUMMARY OF DIVORCE LAWS BY STATE

ALABAMA

Grounds for divorce: Irretrievable breakdown of the marriage; complete incompatibility; adultery; abandonment (one year); nonsupport by husband (two years); imprisonment (two years on a sentence of seven or more years); confinement for insanity (five years); cruelty; alcoholism; drug addiction; incurable impotence; legal separation (two years); wife pregnant by another at time of marriage without husband's knowledge; unnatural sexual behavior before or after marriage.

Residence requirement: Six months.

Alimony and property: Fault is one of the bases on which court determines amount and recipient of support unless the divorce is granted on a "no fault" ground. Only the wife is eligible to receive support. There are no statutory provisions for the division of property.

Wife's name: No statute.

Grounds for judicial separation: Same as the grounds for divorce.

Grounds for annulment: None. However, an incestuous marriage can be voided if either spouse is convicted of that crime.

ALASKA

Grounds for divorce: Incompatibility; adultery; willful desertion (one year); willful neglect by husband (one year); conviction for a felony; insanity (eighteen months); cruel and inhuman treatment; alcoholism (one year); drug addiction; impotence; personal indignities.

Residence requirement: One year.

Alimony and property: Fault is not taken into consideration in court's determination of the amount and recipient of support or the division of property. Either spouse is eligible to receive support or property.

Wife's name: Ex-wife may resume her maiden, name if the court approves.

Grounds for judicial separation: No statute.

Grounds for annulment: Incest; bigamy. The following grounds are valid unless the marital relationship is continued after the ground no longer exists: mental incapacity at time of marriage; under age and without parental approval; fraud; force or duress.

ARIZONA

Grounds for divorce (dissolution): Irretrievable breakdown of the marriage.

Residence requirement: One year.

Alimony and property: Fault is not taken into consideration in court's determination of the amount and recipient of support or the division of property. Either spouse is eligible to receive support or property. Any community property or joint tenancy property not divided is kept by both spouses as tenants in common.

Wife's name: Ex-wife may resume her maiden name if the court approves.

Grounds for judicial separation: Same as the grounds for divorce.

Grounds for annulment: None. However, incestuous and bigamous marriages, or those where one party was without mental capacity at time of marriage, can be voided.

ARKANSAS

Grounds for divorce: Adultery; desertion (one year); willful nonsupport; conviction for a felony; idiocy or insanity (three years); cruel or barbarous treatment endangering the life of the spouse; alcoholism (one year); impotence at time of marriage; separation (three years); personal indignities; bigamy.

Residence requirement: Two months.

Alimony and property: Fault is one of the bases on which court determines amount and recipient of support and division of property. Only the wife is eligible to receive support and property. Spouses may make a contract stipulating alimony payments and distribution of property; if approved by the court, the contract will be enforceable.

Wife's name: Ex-wife may resume her maiden name if the court approves, providing she does not have custody of couple's minor children.

Grounds for judicial separation: No statute.

Grounds for annulment: Mental incapacity at time of marriage; under age; fraud; force or duress; incest; impotence at time of marriage.

CALIFORNIA

Grounds for divorce (dissolution): Irreconcilable differences; incurable insanity.

Residence requirement: Six months in s.ate, three months in county.

Alimony and property: Fault is not taken into consideration in court's determination of the amount and recipient of support or the division of property. Either spouse is eligible to receive support or property. Community property is divided equally. Spouses may make a contract stipulating support payments and distribution of property; if approved by the court, the contract will be enforceable.

Wife's name: Ex-wife may resume her maiden name if the court approves.

Grounds for judicial separation: Same as the grounds for dissolution.

Grounds for annulment: Bigamy; incurable impotence. The following grounds are valid unless the marital relationship is continued after the ground no longer exists: mental incapacity at time of marriage; under age; fraud; force or duress.

COLORADO

Grounds for divorce (dissolution): Irretrievable breakdown of the marriage.

Residence requirement: Ninety days.

Alimony and property: Fault is not taken into consideration in court's determination of the amount and recipient of support or the division of property. Either spouse is eligible to receive support or property. In the division of property, court may give preference to the spouse who has custody of couple's minor children.

Wife's name: No statute.

Grounds for judicial separation: Same as the grounds for divorce.

Grounds for annulment: Mental incapacity at time of marriage, including that caused by drugs or alcohol; fraud; duress; physical inability to perform sexual intercourse; couple got married on a dare or as a jest. Incestuous and bigamous marriages which were void in the states where they were performed may be declared invalid.

CONNECTICUT

Grounds for divorce: Adultery; willful desertion (one year); absence (seven years); conviction for a crime involving violation of conjugal duty and with a sentence of more than one year; life imprisonment; confinement for insanity (five years); intolerable cruelty; alcoholism; fraud.

Residence requirement: None if grounds for divorce occurred in the state or if plaintiff was a resident of state before marriage and returned with the intention of remaining permanently; otherwise, one year.

Alimony and property: Fault is not taken into consideration in court's determination of the amount and recipient of support or the division of property. Either spouse is eligible to receive support or property. Spouses may make a contract stipulating support payments, distribution of property, and child custody and support; if approved by the court, the contract will be enforceable.

Wife's name: Ex-wife may resume her maiden name if the court approves.

Grounds for judicial separation: Same as the grounds for divorce.

Grounds for annulment: None. However, whenever a marriage is void or voidable for any cause under the laws of Connecticut or of the state where the marriage was performed, the marriage may be declared void.

DELAWARE

Grounds for divorce: Incompatibility (two years); adultery; desertion (one year); nonsupport; imprisonment (two years—or, if the sentence is for an indeterminant time, one year); chronic mental illness or epilepsy (five years); extreme cruelty; alcoholism (two years); separation (eighteen months); bigamy; under age.

Residence requirement: One year.

Alimony and property: Fault is not taken into consideration in court's determination of the amount and recipient of support or the division of property. Support will be granted to the defendant in a divorce case based on incompatibility if he or she can prove dependence on the other spouse. Wife may be granted a reasonable share of husband's real and personal property if the divorce is not granted on grounds of incompatibility, voluntary separation, or under age. Spouses may make a contract stipulating support payments and distribution of property;

if approved by the court, the contract will be enforceable.

Wife's name: No statute.

Grounds for judicial separation: No statute.

Grounds for annulment: Bigamy; incest; incurable impotence. The following grounds are valid unless the marital relationship is continued after the ground no longer exists: under age; fraud; force or duress; insanity.

DISTRICT OF COLUMBIA

Grounds for divorce: Adultery; desertion (one year); conviction for a felony with a sentence of at least two years; separation (one year).

Residence requirement: One year.

Alimony and property: Fault is not taken into consideration in court's determination of the amount and recipient of support or the division of property. Only the wife is eligible to receive support, but either spouse may be awarded property. Spouses may make a contract stipulating support payments and distribution of property; if approved by the court, the contract will be enforceable.

Wife's name: No statute.

Grounds for judicial separation: Same as the grounds for divorce, plus cruelty.

Grounds for annulment: Fraud; force or duress; bigamy; impotence. Mental incapacity at time of marriage is valid unless the marital relationship is continued after the ground no longer exists.

FLORIDA

Grounds for divorce (dissolution): Irretrievable breakdown of the marriage; mental incompetence (three years).
Residence requirement: Six months.
Alimony and property: Fault is not taken into consideration in court's determination of the amount and recipient of support. Either spouse is eligible to receive support. There are no statutory provisions for the division of property.
Wife's name: No statute.
Grounds for judicial separation: No statute.
Grounds for annulment: None.

GEORGIA

Grounds for divorce: Adultery; desertion (one year); conviction for a felony involving immoral behavior with a sentence of at least two years; incurable insanity (two years); mental or physical cruelty; alcoholism; drug addiction; impotence at time of marriage; wife pregnant by another at time of marriage without husband's knowledge; fraud; mental incapacity at time of marriage; force or duress; incest.
Grounds for judicial separation: No statute.
Grounds for annulment: None. However, if spouses were incompetent or fraudulently induced to marry, an annulment may be granted unless there are children as a result of the marriage.

HAWAII

Grounds for divorce (dissolution): Irretrievable

breakdown of the marriage; living apart under a decree of separate maintenance (two years).

Residence requirement: One year in state, three months in county.

Alimony and property: Fault is not taken into consideration in court's determination of the amount and recipient of support or the division of property. Either spouse is eligible to receive support or property. Spouses may make a contract stipulating support payments and distribution of property; if approved by the court, the contract will be enforceable.

Wife's name: No statute.

Grounds for judicial separation: Same as the grounds for divorce. There is a two-year limit on the duration of the separation.

Grounds for annulment: Mental incapacity at time of marriage; under age; fraud; force or duress; bigamy; incest; impotence; either spouse afflicted with any loathsome disease if this is unknown to the other.

IDAHO

Grounds for divorce: Irreconcilable differences; adultery; willful desertion; willful neglect; conviction for a felony; permanent insanity; extreme cruelty (bodily injury or mental suffering); alcoholism; living apart (five years).

Residence requirement: Six weeks.

Alimony and property: Fault is one of the bases on which court determines amount and recipient of support unless the divorce is granted on a "no fault" ground. Only the wife is eligible to receive support. Either party may be awarded community property.

Wife's name: No statute.

Grounds for judicial separation: No statute.

Grounds for annulment: Bigamy; incurable impotence. The following grounds are valid unless the marital relationship is continued after the ground no longer exists: mental incapacity at time of marriage; under age; fraud; force.

ILLINOIS

Grounds for divorce: Adultery; desertion (one year); conviction for a felony; attempt on life of spouse; mental or physical cruelty; alcoholism (two years); drug addiction (two years); impotence; bigamy; venereal disease if communicated to spouse.

Residence requirement: Six months if grounds occurred in state; otherwise, one year.

Alimony and property: Fault is not taken into consideration in court's determination of the amount and recipient of support or the division of property. Either spouse is eligible to receive support or property.

Wife's name: Ex-wife may resume her maiden name if the court approves.

Grounds for judicial separation: Permitted if "necessary for health and happiness . . . in addition to disregard of the marital obligations."

Grounds for annulment: Annulment may be granted, but grounds are not enumerated by statute.

INDIANA

Grounds for divorce: Irretrievable breakdown of the marriage; adultery; desertion; conviction for a felony after marriage; incurable insanity (two years); impotence at time of marriage.

Residence requirement: Six months in state, three months in county.

Alimony and property: Fault is not taken into consideration in court's determination of the amount and recipient of support or the division of property. Either spouse is eligible to receive support or property, although court may not award support payments unless the spouse is incapacitated, and then only for the duration of the disability. Spouses may make a contract stipulating support payments, distribution of property, and education and religious training of minor children; if approved by the court, the contract will be enforceable.

Wife's name: Ex-wife may resume her maiden name if the court approves.

Grounds for judicial separation: Adultery; husband's desertion or refusal to provide for wife (six months); cruelty; "intolerable recurring strife"; alcoholism; drug addiction; failure to cohabit (six months).

Residence requirement: Six months.

Alimony and property: Fault is one of the bases on which court determines amount and recipient of support and division of property. Only the wife is eligible to receive support, but either spouse may be awarded property. Spouses may make a contract stipulating support payments and distribution of property; if approved by the court, the contract will be enforceable.

Wife's name: Ex-wife may resume her maiden name or the name of a former husband if the court approves.

Grounds for annulment: Mental incapacity at time of marriage; under age; fraud; bigamy; incest.

IOWA

Grounds for divorce (dissolution): Irretrievable breakdown of the marriage.

Residence requirement: None if both spouses are residents of state; one year if defendant is not a state resident.

Alimony and property: Fault is not taken into consideration in court's determination of the amount and recipient of support or the division of property. Either spouse is eligible to receive support or property.

Wife's name: No statute.

Grounds for judicial separation: Same as the grounds for divorce.

Grounds for annulment: Mental incapacity at time of marriage; impotence at time of marriage; marriage prohibited by law. Bigamy is valid unless the marital relationship is continued after the first marriage is ended.

KANSAS

Grounds for divorce: Incompatibility; adultery; abandonment (one year); gross neglect of duty;

conviction for a felony and imprisonment after marriage; mental illness (three years); extreme cruelty; alcoholism.

Residence requirement: Six months.

Alimony and property: Fault is not taken into consideration in court's determination of the amount and recipient of support or the division of property. Either spouse is eligible to receive support or property.

Wife's name: Ex-wife may resume her maiden name if the court approves.

Grounds for judicial separation: Same as the grounds for divorce.

Grounds for annulment: Fraud; bigamy; impotence at time of marriage; wife pregnant by another at time of marriage without husband's knowledge.

KENTUCKY

Grounds for divorce (dissolution): Irretrievable breakdown of the marriage.

Residence requirement: Six months.

Alimony and property: Fault is not taken into consideration in court's determination of the amount and recipient of support and the division of property. Either spouse is eligible to receive support or property. Spouses may make a contract stipulating support payments and distribution of property; if approved by the court, the contract will be enforceable.

Wife's name: Ex-wife may resume her maiden name or a former husband's name if the court approves.

Grounds for judicial separation: Permitted for "any cause the court deems sufficient."

Grounds for annulment: Mental incapacity at time of marriage, including that caused by drugs or alcohol; fraud; force or duress; physical inability to perform sexual intercourse; marriage prohibited by law.

LOUISIANA

Grounds for divorce: Adultery; conviction for a felony. The following grounds are valid only after a separation and a failure of reconciliation for one year: abandonment; nonsupport; being a fugitive from justice; mental or physical cruelty; attempt on life of spouse; public defamation of spouse.

Residence requirement: None if at least one spouse is domiciled in the state or the grounds occurred there; otherwise, one year.

Alimony and property: Fault is one of the bases on which court determines amount and recipient of support and property. Only the wife is eligible to receive alimony, but either spouse may be awarded property. Community property is divided equally.

Wife's name: No statute.

Grounds for judicial separation: Same as the grounds for divorce.

Grounds for annulment: Duress is valid unless the marital relationship is continued after the ground no longer exists.

MAINE

Grounds for divorce: Irreconcilable differences; adultery; desertion (three years); nonsupport; extreme cruelty; cruel or abusive treatment; alcoholism; drug addicition; impotence.

Residence requirement: None if spouses were married in the state or cohabited there after marriage, the plaintiff resided in the state when the grounds occurred, or the defendant is a resident; otherwise, six months.

Alimony and property: Fault is one of the bases on which court determines amount and recipient of support and division of property unless the divorce is granted on a "no fault" ground. Only the wife is eligible to receive support, but either spouse may be awarded property.

Wife's name: Ex-wife may resume her maiden name if the court approves.

Grounds for judicial separation: Desertion (one year); living apart for a justifiable reason (one year).

Grounds for annulment: Mental incapacity at time of marriage; bigamy; incest; life imprisonment.

MARYLAND

Grounds for divorce: Adultery; abandonment (one year); imprisonment for at least three years, eighteen months of which must have been served by the time the suit is filed; incurable insanity (three years); impotence at time of marriage; separation (one year); voluntarily living apart (three years).

Residence requirement: None if grounds occurred within the state; otherwise, one year.

Alimony and property: Fault is one of the bases on which court determines amount and recipient of support and division of property. Either spouse is eligible to receive support or property, but support is absolutely barred to a spouse guilty of adultery.

Wife's name: Ex-wife may resume her maiden name if the court approves.

Grounds for judicial separation: Abandonment; desertion; cruelty; "excessively vicious conduct"; living apart without hope of reconciliation.

Grounds for annulment: Incest; bigamy.

MASSACHUSETTS

Grounds for divorce: Adultery; desertion (two years); nonsupport; conviction for a felony with a sentence of at least five years; physical cruelty; alcoholism; drug addiction; impotence.

Residence requirement: None if the couple lived in the state or if the plaintiff is a resident and grounds occurred there; otherwise, two years.

Alimony and property: Fault is not taken into consideration in court's determination of the not divided is kept by both spouses as tenants in common.

Wife's name: Ex-wife may resume her maiden name or a former husband's name if the court approves.

Grounds for judicial separation: Same as the grounds for divorce.

Grounds for annulment: Mental incapacity at

time of marriage; fraud; bigamy; incest. The following grounds are valid unless the marital relationship is continued after the ground no longer exists: under age; force or duress.

MICHIGAN

Grounds for divorce (dissolution): Irretrievable breakdown of the marriage.

Residence requirement: None if the couple was married in the state and resided there continuously; otherwise, one year.

Alimony and property: Fault is not taken into consideration in court's determination of the amount and recipient of support or the division of property. Either spouse is eligible to receive support or property. Any joint tenancy property amount and recipient of support or the division of property. Either spouse is eligible to receive support or property. Any joint tenancy property not divided is kept by both spouses as tenants in common. Spouses may make a contract stipulating support payments and distribution of property; if approved by the court, the contract will be enforceable.

Wife's name: Ex-wife may resume her maiden name if the court approves.

Grounds for judicial separation: Desertion; husband's failure to support wife; living apart for a justifiable reason.

Grounds for annulment: Mental incapacity at time of marriage; under age; bigamy; incest.

MINNESOTA

Grounds for divorce: Adultery; desertion (one

year); imprisonment after marriage; insanity (three years); alcoholism (one year); impotence; separation under a decree of limited divorce (five years); separation following a decree of separate maintenance (two years); course of conduct detrimental to the marriage.

Residence requirement: None for adultery; for other grounds, one year.

Alimony and property: Fault is not taken into consideration in court's determination of the amount and recipient of support or the division of property. Either spouse is eligible to receive support or property.

Wife's name: Ex-wife may resume her maiden name if the court approves.

Grounds for judicial separation: No statute.

Grounds for annulment: Mental incapacity at time of marriage; under age; fraud; force; bigamy; incest.

MISSISSIPPI

Grounds for divorce: Adultery; desertion (one year); conviction for a felony; incurable insanity (three years); habitual cruel and inhumane treatment; alcoholism; drug addiction; impotence; wife pregnant by another at time of marriage without husband's knowledge; insanity at time of marriage without other spouse's knowledge; mental incapacity at time of marriage; incest.

Residence requirement: One year.

Alimony and property: Fault is not taken into consideration in court's determination of the amount and recipient of support. Only the wife

96

is eligible to receive support. There are no statutory provisions for division of property, except that joint tenancy is not affected by the divorce.

Wife's name: No statute.

Grounds for judicial separation: No statute.

Grounds for annulment: Mental incapacity at time of marriage; under age; fraud; bigamy; incest; impotence at time of marriage; failure to obtain marriage license; insanity at time of marriage; wife pregnant by another at time of marriage without husband's knowledge.

MISSOURI

Grounds for divorce (dissolution): Irretrievable breakdown of the marriage.

Residence requirement: One spouse must be a resident of the state or a member of the armed forces stationed there for at least ninety days.

Alimony and property: Fault is not taken into consideration in court's determination of the amount and recipient of support or the division of property. Either spouse is eligible to receive support or property. Spouses may make a contract stipulating support payments, distribution of property, and child custody, support, and visitation rights; if approved by the court, the contract will be enforceable.

Wife's name: No statute.

Grounds for judicial separation: No statute.

Grounds for annulment: None. However, incestuous and bigamous marriages, or those where one spouse was without mental capacity at time of marriage or a license was not obtained, are void.

MONTANA

Grounds for divorce: Adultery; willful desertion (one year); willful neglect (one year); conviction for a felony; incurable insanity (five years); extreme physical or mental cruelty, including false charges of unchastity (mental cruelty must continue for one year); alcoholism (one year).

Residence requirement: One year.

Alimony and property: Fault is one of the bases on which court determines amount and recipient of support and division of property. Only the wife is eligible to receive support, but either spouse may be awarded property. Spouses may make a contract stipulating support payments and distribution of property; if approved by the court, the contract will be enforceable.

Wife's name: No statute.

Grounds for judicial separation: Same as the grounds for divorce.

Grounds for annulment: Bigamy; incest; physical inability to perform sexual intercourse. The following grounds are valid unless the marital relationship is continued after the ground no longer exists: lack of mental capacity at time of marriage; under.age; fraud; force.

NEBRASKA

Grounds for divorce (dissolution): Irretrievable breakdown of the marriage.

Residence requirement: One year if couple was married in the state and resided there continuously during their marriage.

Alimony and property: Fault is not taken into consideration in court's determination of the amount and recipient of support or the division of property. Either spouse is eligible to receive support or property. Spouses may make a contract stipulating support payments, distribution of property, and child custody and support; if approved by the court, the contract will be enforceable.

Wife's name: No statute.

Grounds for judicial separation: No statute.

Grounds for annulment: Mental illness or retardation at time of marriage; fraud; force; bigamy; impotence at time of marriage; marriage prohibited by law.

NEVADA

Grounds for divorce: Incompatibility; adultery; desertion (one year); nonsupport by husband when he was capable of providing for wife (one year); conviction for a felony; insanity (two years); extreme cruelty; alcoholism; impotence at time of marriage and continuing to time of divorce; separation (one year).

Residence requirement: Six weeks.

Alimony and property: Fault is not taken into consideration in court's determination of the amount and recipient of support or the division of property. Only the wife is eligible to receive support and part of husband's separate property, but either spouse may be awarded community property. Spouses may make a contract stipulating support payments, distribution of property, and child custody and support; if approved by the court, the contract will be enforceable.

Wife's name: Ex-wife may resume her maiden name if the court approves.

Grounds for judicial separation: No statute.

Grounds for annulment: Bigamy; incest. The following grounds are valid unless the marital relationship is continued after the ground no longer exists: mental incapacity at time of marriage; under age; fraud.

NEW HAMPSHIRE

Grounds for divorce: Irreconcilable differences; adultery; abandonment (two years); nonsupport by husband (two years); refusal to cohabit (two years); wife's absence without husband's consent (two years); wife out of state without husband's consent (ten years); husband becoming a citizen of a foreign country without leaving wife any means of support; imprisonment (at least one year); extreme cruelty; alcoholism; impotence; refusing to live together (six months); joining a religion which believes marital relations are immoral.

Residence requirement: None if both spouses are residents of the state or the plaintiff is a resident and defendant was personally served notice within the state; otherwise, one year.

Alimony and property: Fault is one of the bases on which court determines amount and recipient of support and division of property unless divorce is granted on a "no fault" ground. Only the wife is eligible to receive support and property.

Wife's name: Wife may resume her maiden name if the court approves.

Grounds for judicial separation: Same as the grounds for divorce.

Grounds for annulment: Being under age is valid unless the marital relationship is continued after the ground no longer exists. Incestuous and bigamous marriages are void.

NEW JERSEY

Grounds for divorce: Adultery; desertion (one year); imprisonment (eighteen months); confinement for mental illness (two years); physical or mental cruelty; alcoholism (one year); drug addiction (one year); separation without prospect of reconciliation (eighteen months); deviant sexual conduct without other spouse's approval.

Residence requirement: None for adultery; for other grounds, one year.

Alimony and property: Fault is one of the bases on which court determines amount and recipient of support and division of property. Either spouse is eligible to receive support or property.

Wife's name: Ex-wife may resume her maiden name if the court approves. Also, the court may rule that the wife may *not* use her ex-husband's name.

Grounds for judicial separation: Same as the grounds for divorce.

Grounds for annulment: Incest; bigamy; impotence at time of marriage without other spouse's knowledge. The following grounds are valid unless the marital relationship is continued after the ground no longer exists: mental incapacity at time of marriage, including that caused by drugs or alcohol; under age; duress; fraud.

NEW MEXICO

Grounds for divorce: Incompatibility; adultery; abandonment; cruel and inhumane treatment.
Residence requirement: Six months.
Alimony and property: Fault is not taken into consideration in court's determination of the amount and recipient of support. Either spouse is eligible to receive support. There are no statutory provisions for the basis on which property is divided because the decree may not include a division of property; proceedings may be instituted later to have it divided, however. Spouses may make a contract stipulating support payments and distribution of property; if approved by the court, the contract will be enforceable.
Wife's name: Ex-wife may resume her maiden name if the court approves.
Grounds for judicial separation: Living apart without hope of reconciliation.
Grounds for annulment: Under age. Incestuous and bigamous marriages are void.

NEW YORK

Grounds for divorce: Adultery; abandonment (one year); imprisonment after marriage (three years); mental or physical cruelty; legal separation (one year).
Residence requirement: None if couple was married in the state, at least one spouse was resident

when grounds occurred, and both are residents at time of suit; otherwise, one year or—if neither marriage nor grounds occurred in state—two years.

Alimony and property: Fault is one of the bases on which court determines amount and recipient of support and division of property. Only wife is eligible to receive alimony and property.

Wife's name: No statute.

Grounds for judicial separation: Same as the grounds for divorce, plus husband's failure to support wife.

Grounds for annulment: Mental incapacity at time of marriage; under age; fraud; impotence; insanity (five years).

NORTH CAROLINA

Grounds for divorce: Adultery; desertion; insanity (three years); impotence at time of marriage; separation (one year); wife pregnant by another at time of marriage without husband's knowledge; unnatural or abnormal sex act.

Residence requirement: Six months.

Alimony and property: Fault is one of the bases on which court determines amount and recipient of alimony. Either spouse is eligible to receive support, but it is absolutely barred to a spouse guilty of adultery. There are no statutory provisions for the basis on which property is divided.

Wife's name: Ex-wife may resume her maiden name or a former dead husband's name if the court approves.

Grounds for judicial separation: Abandonment; cruel and barbarous treatment endangering life;

"indignities to the person"; alcoholism; drug addiction; one partner "maliciously turning the other out of the home."

Grounds for annulment: Mental incapacity at time of marriage; under age; bigamy; incest; impotence.

NORTH DAKOTA

Grounds for divorce: Irreconcilable differences; adultery; willful desertion; willful neglect; conviction for a felony; insanity (five years); extreme cruelty; alcoholism.

Residence requirement: One year.

Alimony and property: Fault is not taken into consideration in court's determination of the amount and recipient of support or the division of property. Either spouse is eligible to receive support or property.

Wife's name: Ex-wife may resume her maiden name if the court approves.

Grounds for judicial separation: Same as the grounds for divorce.

Grounds for annulment: Bigamy; incest; impotence at time of marriage that seems incurable. The following grounds are valid unless the marital relationship is continued after the ground no longer exists: mental incapacity at time of marriage; under age; fraud; force or duress.

OHIO

Grounds for divorce: Adultery; willful neglect (one year); willful absence (one year); conviction for a felony if imprisoned at time of suit; extreme cruelty; alcoholism (one year); impotence; bigamy; fraud; successful attempt to obtain divorce in another state.

Residence requirement: One year.

Alimony and property: Fault is one of the bases on which court determines amount and recipient of support and division of property. Either spouse is eligible to receive support or property.

Wife's name: Ex-wife may resume her maiden name if the court approves.

Grounds for judicial separation: No statute.

Grounds for annulment: Bigamy; unconsummated marriage. The following grounds are valid unless the marital relationship is continued after the ground no longer exists: mental incapacity at time of marriage; under age; fraud; force or duress. Incestuous marriages are void.

OKLAHOMA

Grounds for divorce: Incompatibility; adultery; abandonment (one year); gross neglect; conviction for a felony if imprisoned at time of suit; insanity (five years); extreme cruelty; alcoholism; impotence; wife pregnant by another at time of marriage; fraud; divorce obtained outside of state but not recognized in state.

Residence requirement: Six months.

Alimony and property: Fault is one of the bases on which court determines amount and recipient of support and division of property unless the divorce is granted on a "no fault" ground. Only the wife is eligible to receive support, but either spouse may be awarded property.

Wife's name: Ex-wife may resume her maiden name if approved by the court, providing her husband was at fault in the divorce.

Grounds for judicial separation: Same as the grounds for divorce.

Grounds for annulment: Mental incapacity at time of marriage and being under age are valid unless the marital relationship is continued after the ground no longer exists. Incestuous and bigamous marriages are void.

OREGON

Grounds for divorce (dissolution): Irretrievable breakdown of the marriage; irreconcilable differences.

Residence requirement: None if couple was married in the state and one spouse is resident there; otherwise, six months.

Alimony and property: Fault is not taken into consideration in court's determination of the amount and recipient of support or the division of property. Either spouse is eligible to receive support or property. Any joint tenancy property not divided is kept by both spouses as tenants in common. Spouses may make a contract stipulating support payments and distribution of property; if approved by the court, the contract will be enforceable.

Wife's name: Ex-wife may resume her maiden name if the court approves.

Grounds for judicial separation: Same as the grounds for divorce.

Grounds for annulment: Mental incapacity at

time of marriage; under age; fraud; bigamy; incest; force or duress.

PENNSYLVANIA

Grounds for divorce: Adultery; desertion (two years); conviction for a felony (two years); insanity (three years); physical cruelty; impotence at time of marriage; inability to procreate at time of marriage; bigamy; fraud; personal indignities; force or coercion; incest.

Residence requirement: One year.

Alimony and property: Fault is one of the bases on which court determines amount and recipient of support, but there are no statutory provisions to grant it except to a wife during a legal separation or to either spouse if the divorce was granted on grounds of insanity and the insane person's estate is not sufficient to provide his or her support. There are no statutory provisions for the basis on which property is divided, but any joint tenancy property not divided is kept by both spouses as tenants in common.

Wife's name: No statute.

Grounds for judicial separation: Adultery; abandonment; cruel and barbarous treatment; being turned out of the home; personal indignities. May be obtained only by the wife.

Grounds for annulment: Mental incapacity at time of marriage; bigamy; incest.

RHODE ISLAND

Grounds for divorce: Adultery; desertion (five years—or less at discretion of court); nonsupport;

life imprisonment if person is considered legally dead; extreme cruelty; alcoholism; drug addiction; voluntarily living apart; bigamy; gross misbehavior; mental incapacity at time of marriage; incest.

Residence requirement: Two years.

Alimony and property: Fault is one of the bases on which court determines amount and recipient of support and division of property. Only the wife is eligible to receive support, but only if she has waived her dower rights, to which she is entitled upon divorce. Either spouse is eligible to receive property.

Wife's name: Ex-wife may resume her maiden name if the court approves.

Grounds for judicial separation: Same as the grounds for divorce.

Grounds for annulment: None. However, incestuous and bigamous marriages, or those where there was mental incapacity at the time of marriage, are void.

SOUTH CAROLINA

Grounds for divorce: Adultery; desertion (one year); physical cruelty; alcoholism; drug addiction; separation (three years).

Residence requirement: One year.

Alimony and property: Fault is one of the bases on which court determines amount and recipient of support. Only the wife is eligible to receive support, but it is absolutely barred to her if she is guilty of adultery. There are no statutory provisions for the basis on which property is divided.

Wife's name: Ex-wife may resume her maiden name if the court approves.

Grounds for judicial separation: No statute.

Grounds for annulment: Mental incapacity at time of marriage; duress; bigamy; marriage not consummated.

SOUTH DAKOTA

Grounds for divorce: Adultery; desertion (one year); willful neglect (one year); conviction for a felony; insanity (five years—or less at discretion of court); physical or mental cruelty; alcoholism (one year).

Residence requirement: None if couple was married in state and plaintiff still resides there; otherwise, one year in state, three months in county.

Alimony and property: Fault is one of the bases on which court determines amount and recipient of support but it is not considered in the division of property. Only the wife is eligible to receive support, but either spouse may be awarded property.

Wife's name: Ex-wife may resume her maiden name if the court approves, providing she does not have custody of couple's minor children.

Grounds for judicial separation: Same as the grounds for divorce.

Grounds for annulment: Under age; bigamy; impotence at time of marriage which appears to be incurable. The following grounds are valid unless the marital relationship is continued after the ground no longer exists: mental incapacity; fraud; force or duress. Incestuous marriages are void.

TENNESSEE

Grounds for divorce: Adultery; abandonment; neglect; cruel and inhuman treatment; indignities.

Residence requirement: One year.

Alimony and property: Fault is one of the bases on which court determines amount and recipient of support but it is not considered in the division of property. Only the wife is eligible to receive support, but either spouse may be awarded property. Spouses may make a contract stipulating support payments and distribution of property; if approved by the court, the contract will be enforceable.

Wife's name: No statute.

Grounds for judicial separation: Same as the grounds for divorce.

Grounds for annulment: Mental incapacity at time of marriage; under age; fraud; force or duress; bigamy; incest.

TEXAS

Grounds for divorce: Irretrievable breakdown of the marriage.

Residence requirement: One year in state, six months in county.

Alimony and property: Fault is not taken into consideration in court's determination of the division of property.

Wife's name: Ex-wife may resume her maiden name if the court approves.

Grounds for judicial separation: No statute.

Grounds for annulment: Under the influence of

drugs or alcohol at time of marriage; under age; marriage within six months of a previous divorce. The following grounds are valid unless the marital relationship is continued after the ground no longer exists: lack of mental capacity at time of marriage; fraud; force or duress; impotence at time of marriage. Incestuous and bigamous marriages are void.

UTAH

Grounds for divorce: Adultery; desertion (one year); willful neglect; conviction for a felony; insanity; mental or physical cruelty; alcoholism; impotence at time of marriage; separation (three years).
Residence requirement: Three months.
Alimony and property: Fault is not taken into consideration in court's determination of the amount and recipient of support or the division of property. Either spouse is eligible to receive support or property.
Wife's name: Ex-wife may resume her maiden name if the court approves.
Grounds for judicial separation: Abandonment; desertion; neglect. May be obtained only by the wife.
Grounds for annulment: Mental incapacity at time of marriage; under age; force or duress; incest; marriage not officially solemnized; venereal disease; previous divorce not final.

VERMONT

Grounds for divorce: Adultery; willful desertion; nonsupport; absence for seven years without news; conviction for a felony with a sentence of at least three years; incurable insanity (five years); intolerable severity; separation (six months).

Residence requirement: Six months.

Alimony and property: Fault is not taken into consideration in court's determination of the amount and recipient of support or the division of property. Either spouse is eligible to receive support, but only the wife may be awarded property.

Wife's name: Ex-wife may resume her maiden name or a former husband's name if the court approves.

Grounds for judicial separation: Same as the grounds for divorce.

Grounds for annulment: Mental incapacity at time of marriage; fraud; force; impotence (one year). Being under age is valid unless the marital relationship is continued after the ground no longer exists. Incestuous and bigamous marriages are void.

VIRGINIA

Grounds for divorce: Adultery; abandonment (one year); desertion (one year); imprisonment; impotence at time of marriage; separation (two years); wife pregnant by another at time of marriage without husband's knowledge; sodomy or buggery; either spouse convicted of a felony before marriage without the other's knowledge; wife a prostitute before marriage without husband's knowledge.

Residence requirement: One year.

Alimony and property: Fault is one of the bases on which court determines amount and recipient of support. Either spouse is eligible to receive support. There are no statutory provisions for the basis on which property is divided, but any joint tenancy property not divided is kept by both spouses as tenants in common. Spouses may make a contract stipulating support payments, distribution of property, and child custody and support; if approved by the court, the contract will be enforceable.

Wife's name: No statute.

Grounds for judicial separation: Abandonment; desertion; cruelty; fear of bodily harm.

Grounds for annulment: Mental incapacity at time of marriage; under age; fraud; force or duress; incest; impotence; malformation preventing sexual intercourse; marriage not officially solemnized.

WASHINGTON

Grounds for divorce (dissolution): Irretrievable breakdown of the marriage.

Residence requirement: Six months.

Alimony and property: Fault is not taken into consideration in court's determination of the amount and recipient of support or the division of property. Either spouse is eligible to receive support or property.

Wife's name: Ex-wife may resume her maiden name if the court approves.

Grounds for judicial separation: No statute.

Grounds for annulment: Under age; fraud; bigamy; incest.

WEST VIRGINIA

Grounds for divorce: Adultery; desertion (one year); abandonment (one year); insanity (three years); mental or physical cruelty; alcoholism after marriage; drug addiction after marriage; separation (two years).

Residence requirement: None for adultery if defendant can be served notice personally; otherwise, and for other grounds, one year.

Alimony and property: Fault is one of the bases on which court determines amount and recipient of support and division of property. Either spouse is eligible to receive support or property.

Wife's name: Ex-wife may resume her maiden name, providing she does not have custody of couple's minor children.

Grounds for judicial separation: No statute.

Grounds for annulment: The following grounds are valid unless the marital relationship is continued after the ground no longer exists: mental incapacity at time of marriage; under age; fraud; force or duress; bigamy; incest; impotence; malformation preventing sexual intercourse; wife pregnant by another at time of marriage; venereal disease at time of marriage; conviction for a serious crime before marriage without spouse's knowledge; wife a prostitute before marriage without husband's knowledge; husband known to be immoral before marriage without wife's knowledge.

WISCONSIN

Grounds for divorce: Adultery; desertion (one

year); nonsupport; conviction for a felony with a sentence of at least three years; voluntary commitment to a mental institution (one year); mental or physical cruelty; alcoholism (one year); separation (one year); court decree of separate maintenance (one year).

Residence requirement: Six months in state, one month in county.

Alimony and property: Fault is one of the bases on which court determines amount and recipient of support but it is not considered in the division of property. Either spouse is eligible to receive support or property, but support is absolutely barred to a spouse guilty of adultery.

Wife's name: Ex-wife may resume her maiden name or a former husband's name if the court approves, providing she does not have custody of the couple's minor children.

Grounds for judicial separation: Same as the grounds for divorce.

Grounds for annulment: Mental incapacity at time of marriage; under age; fraud; force or duress; bigamy; incest; impotence; inability to perform sexual intercourse; marriage within six months of previous divorce.

WYOMING

Grounds for divorce: Incompatibility; adultery; desertion (one year); nonsupport (one year); vagrancy; conviction for a felony; insanity (two years); mental or physical cruelty; alcoholism; impotence; separation (two years); wife pregnant by another at time of marriage without husband's knowledge.

Residence requirement: Two months.

Alimony and property: Fault is not taken into consideration in court's determination of the amount and recipient of support or the division of property. Only the wife is eligible to receive support and property. Spouses may make a contract stipulating support payments and distribution of property; if approved by the court, the contract will be enforceable.

Wife's name: Ex-wife may resume her maiden name if the court approves.

Grounds for judicial separation: Same as the grounds for divorce.

Grounds for annulment: Mental incapacity at time of marriage; bigamy; incest. The following grounds are valid unless the marital relationship is continued after the ground no longer exists: under age; fraud; force or duress.

GLOSSARY

ABANDONMENT--the withdrawal from the performance of marital obligations or the denial of marital rights without just cause. This may be a physical separation and leaving of the home and the spouse or a "constructive abandonment" by remaining in the home but denying the spouse the physical rights of marital relations.

ADULTERY--the voluntary sexual intercourse of a married person with a person of the opposite sex other than the offender's husband or wife (in some jurisdictions adultery is committed only when the woman is married, while in other jurisdictions, both partners in the sexual act are guilty and in still other jurisdictions, notably New York State since September 1, 1967, "deviate sexual intercourse" with any person other than the spouse--whether of the same or opposite sex--constitutes adultery).

ALIMONY--payments made by one spouse for the support of the other (usually by the husband for the support of the wife, but occasionally by the wife for the support of the husband).

ALIMONY PENDENTE LITE or TEMPORARY ALIMONY--payments made by one spouse for the support of the other between the institution or commencement of the action and the trial and entry of a final judgment of separation, annulment, or divorce. Also referred to as "temporary alimony."

ANNULMENT--the rendering void of a marriage retrospectively as well as prospectively. Distinguished from divorce in that a "divorce action" is based upon a valid marriage and judgment of divorce terminates the marriage from the date of the judgment, while an "annulment" destroys the existence

117

ANNULMENT (continued)--of a void or voidable marriage from the beginning. Note: a judgment of annulment in most jurisdictions does not render the children illegitimate.

ANSWER (oral or written)--the defendant in a law suit attempts to resist the plaintiff's demand, either by denying the allegations of the plaintiff's complaint or by admitting them and alleging new matters in defense or avoidance which the defendant claims should present a recovery by the plaintiff or should give the plaintiff a recovery on his counterclaim.

ANTE-NUPTIAL AGREEMENT--an agreement made between two persons in contemplation of marriage, settling rights which will accrue upon marriage.

BIGAMY--the criminal offense of willfully and knowingly contracting a second marriage (or going through the form of a second marriage ceremony) while the first marriage, to the knowledge of the offender, is still subsisting and undissolved.

BIGAMOUS MARRIAGE--a marriage ceremony or a marriage attempted to be contracted while one of the partners still has a spouse living under a valid marriage which has not been dissolved.

BILL OF PARTICULARS--a written statement or specification of the details or particulars of the complaint or demand for which an action at law is brought. A bill of particulars may be demanded of a complaint, an answer or a counterclaim, seeking further details of the broad statements made in the principal pleading.

COMMON LAW HUSBAND OR WIFE--a man or woman who was a party to a "common law marriage" or one who, having lived with a man or woman in a relation of cohabitation during his or her life, asserts a claim after death of the partner to have been the husband or wife according to the requirements of the common law.

118

COMMON LAW MARRIAGE--a marriage not solemnized by a formal ceremony but created by an agreement or meeting of the minds of a man and woman to marry, followed by cohabitation and by their holding themselves out as husband and wife. May be contracted only by two persons each of whom is free to marry.

CRUEL AND INHUMAN TREATMENT--such barbarous cruelty or severity as endangers the life or health of the party to whom it is addressed or creates a well-founded fear of such danger.

CRUELTY--the intentional and malicious infliction of physical or mental suffering carried to such an extent to make cohabitation unbearable.

CRUELTY, EXTREME--harsh and barbarous treatment of such severity as to be intolerable to any normal human being.

CRUELTY, INTOLERABLE--treatment or a course of conduct willfully and intentionally exercised or practiced, rendering further cohabitation unsafe and impossible.

CRUELTY, MENTAL--severe, willful and malicious conduct which endangers the mental and physical health of a spouse to such an extent as to render continuation of the marriage relationship unbearable, although not accompanied by physical force or violence.

COMPLAINT--the first pleading in an action at law or equity, containing the title of the case, the name of the Court, the names of the parties and a plain and concise statement of the facts upon which the plaintiff relies in asking the Court for relief or judgment.

DECISION--the finding of the Court, setting forth orally or in writing the facts as determined by the Court from the evidence and the conclusions of laws applicable to the case.

DECLARATORY JUDGMENT--a judgment order or decree by a Court defining the rights and status of the parties.

DECREE--a final order or judgment rendered by a Court after a trial or an inquest. The decree may be interlocutory or final.

DESERTION--the act by which a spouse abandons and forsakes the other spouse without justification and without authorization or permission.

DIVISIBLE DIVORCE--a divorce regulating the relationship between a husband and wife but not effecting a total adjudication of all rights and obligations. A divisible divorce may be valid for some purposes but not binding for others.

DIVORCE--the judgment of a Court terminating the marriage relation previously existing between a man and a woman.

FOREIGN DIVORCE--a judgment of divorce rendered by any other state or country.

G.I. MARRIAGE--marriage of a person in military service.

INCEST--sexual intercourse between persons related by blood within varying degrees of kindred. The definition varies from state to state.

INCESTUOUS MARRIAGE--a marriage between a man and woman so closely related by blood as to be prohibited by law. Varies from state to state.

JUDGMENT--an order of a Court made after a trial or hearing permitting the plaintiff to have a money judgment or to be relieved of certain responsibilities or to enforce certain responsibilities.

JUDGMENT OF NULLITY--a judgment declaring that what was a marriage or was purported to be a marriage no longer exists as such. Usually used to declare the nullity of a

JUDGMENT OF NULLITY (continued)--void marriage, although sometimes applied to voidable marriages.

JURISDICTION--the power to make a vinding judgment or order.

JURISDICTION IN PERSONAM--the power to make an order or judgment binding on a person.

JURISDICTION IN REM--the power to make an order or judgment binding on a status or on a particular tangible or intangible thing.

MARRIAGE--the civil status, condition and relation of one man and one woman united in law for life for the discharge to each other and to the community of the duties toward each other and toward the community.

MARRIAGE BY CONTRACT OR CONTRACT MARRIAGE--a marriage performed or consummated without ceremony but by a written instrument signed and acknowledged by each of the parties.

MARRIAGE BY PROXY OR PROXY MARRIAGE--a marriage at which one of the parties is not physically present and is represented by a substitute empowered by written instrument to give a binding consent.

MARRIAGE LICENSE--a certificate or document issued by a governmental authority permitting a man and a woman to enter into the marriage relationship and to participate in a marriage ceremony.

MEDICAL CERTIFICATE--a certification by a physician that a person meets the physical requirements for the issuance of a marriage license.

MISCEGENOUS MARRIAGE--a marriage between two persons of different races forbidden by the law of the jurisdiction in which the marriage has taken place.

121

RESIDENCE REQUIREMENT FOR MARRIAGE--the necessity of residing in a jurisdiction for a period of time prior to the issuance of a marriage license.

RESIDENCE REQUIREMENT FOR A DIVORCE, SEPARATION, OR ANNULMENT--the statute or rule demanding residence for a minimum period before applying to the Court for relief by way of annulment, separation, or divorce.

VOID MARRIAGE--a marriage which is invalid from its inception by reason of lack of capacity of a party to the marriage or some impediment which in effect prohibited the performance of a marriage ceremony.

VOIDABLE MARRIAGE--a marriage which can be annulled or set aside at the election of a party injured by prior conduct or concealment of the spouse, but which will remain in existence unless the injured party moves for relief.

WAITING PERIOD--a mandatory delay following the issuance of a license or following the issuance of a medical certificate during which the parties to whom the license or certificate has been issued may not participate in a marriage ceremony.

WAIVER OF WAITING PERIOD--a dispensation given by a judge or other official permitting parties to marry notwithstanding the requirement that there be a delay following the issuance of a license or medical certificate.

INDEX

Alimony
    enforcement of, 45
    garnishee, 46
    in general, 41-44
    jails, 49
    modification of, 49
    money judgment, 45-46
    sequestration, 46
    security for, 47-48
    see, Appendix E
Annulment
    fraud, 13
    grounds for, 12-13
    see, Appendix E
Ante-nuptial agreements, 1-3

Divorce,
    grounds for, 25-30
    out-of-state & foreign
    decrees, 31-36
    residence requirements, 22
    see, Appendix E

Marriage
    age of consent, 9 (see
    Appendix D)
    ceremony of, 10-11
    common law, 6-7
    consanguinity, 9-10 (see,
    Appendix C)
    consent as element, 5
    definition of, 4

    methods for taking place, 5
    mixed marriages, 10
    persons performing, 5
    restraints upon, 7-8
    void marriages, 8, 12
    voidable marriages, 8-9 (see,
    Appendices A & B)
Military personnel
    in general, 50-51
    residence factors, 52-53
    service of process, 53

Procedures
    choosing attorney, 55
    conference preparation, 56
    fees & costs, 60
    taking action, 57-60

Remarriage, 37-40

Separation
    agreements, 18-20
    costs of, 21
    different from divorce &
    annulment, 14
    effect of reconciliation, 20
    grounds for, 15
    judgment of, 15
    kinds of, 14
    violation of, 14
    see, Appendix E